Sugar Glider

Sugar Gliders As Pets

Sugar Gliders book for care, feeding, diet, health and costs.

By

Celeste Truman

ALL RIGHTS RESERVED. This book contains material protected under International and Federal Copyright Laws and Treaties.

Any unauthorized reprint or use of this material is strictly prohibited. No part of this book may be reproduced or transmitted in any form or by any means, electronic, mechanical or otherwise, including photocopying or recording, or by any information storage and retrieval system without express written permission from the author.

Copyright © 2017

Published by: Zoodoo Publishing

Table of Contents

Table of Contents 3

Introduction 4

Chapter 1: Sugar Gliders - The Basics 5

Chapter 2. Preparing for your Sugar Glider 10

Chapter 3. Coming Home 22

Chapter 4. Day to day life with your Sugar Glider 24

Chapter 5. Making a comfortable habitat for your sugar glider 29

Chapter 6. Sugar Glider behavior and handling 36

Chapter 7. Feeding your sugar glider 39

Chapter 8. Play and Exercise 47

Chapter 9. Hygiene 52

Chapter 10: Health 54

Chapter 11. Diseases that afflict your Sugar Glider 82

Chapter 12. Internet Resources 90

Introduction

Sugar gliders are amongst the most unique pets in the world. They are the only common pet mammal native to Australia. Like so many other species native to Australia, they are also marsupials- a unique group of mammals that give live birth early in the development of their babies, only to have their babies finish development in an external pouch.

Like many of the more famous marsupials of Australia (Kangaroos, Koalas, Wombats, etc.)- they are found nowhere else in the world. Their unique background requires a unique approach to care to adequately rear sugar gliders as pets. We hope the information you find within these pages will help demystify their needs and lead to many happy years of sugar glider ownership.

Chapter 1: Sugar Gliders - The Basics

Although you may have experience in owning other small mammals, sugar gliders have important differences from other common small pets. To better understand, and therefore, better care for your sugar glider it is important to do adequate research into exactly what a sugar glider is, and what it needs to have a happy life.

Understanding your Sugar Glider

Sugar gliders are not closely related to more common household small pets, such as guinea pigs or hamsters. Those small pets (which includes but is not limited to guinea pigs, hamsters, mice, ferrets, etc.) all fall under the subdivision of mammals that are called 'placental mammals'- meaning all development occurs within the womb with the fetus subsisting off the nutrients provided by the (indeed, temporary) placenta organ. In fact, you as a human (being a placental mammal yourself) are more closely related to any other placental mammal than you are to any marsupial, with the last common ancestor between the two divisions of mammals having lived over 100 million years ago- firmly during the age of the dinosaurs!

Despite the vast gulf in time and evolution between you and your sugar glider, they need the same things as any other pet. They need a caring, well-informed owner, proper housing, proper nutrition, adequate veterinary care and an understanding of their basic nature. We will start with a general background to your sugar glider.

Natural history and habitat of sugar gliders
There are a variety of marsupial gliders native to Australia- 6 species to be precise. They are as follows:

- Greater Glider (Petauroides volans)
- Yellow-bellied Glider (Petaurus australis)
- Mahogany Glider (Petaurus gracilis)
- Squirrel Glider (Petaurus norfolcensis)
- Sugar Glider (Petaurus breviceps)
- Feathertail Glider (Acrobates pygmaeus)

All share the same continent, but only the Sugar Glider has ever been adopted en masse as a pet. The above list is also in descending order, going from the largest glider to the smallest- as you can see; the familiar Sugar Glider is the 2nd smallest species of marsupial glider native to Australia.

The Sugar Glider is also native to the island of New Guinea, to Australia's north. This island is divided between the nations of Indonesia (the western half being a province) and Papua New Guinea (being an independent country that constitutes the eastern half of the island). Here it shares its range with two other marsupial gliders:

- Biak Glider (Petaurus biancensis)
- Northern Glider (Petaurus abidi)

Being present over such a wide range, an area roughly contiguous with Eastern and Northern Australia as well as all of New Guinea, there are many noted subspecies, although there is considerable scientific debate whether the populations are distinct enough to warrant such division and labelling. In order to keep the reading light fare, we won't go into any detail about scientific minutiae- not when you're so excited about having such an adorable pet!

The earliest Sugar Glider fossils ever discovered were in the southern Australian State of Victoria and date back to about 15,000 years ago. The Latin name *Petaurus breviceps* translates into English as "Short-headed rope dancer"- no doubt a keen observation as to the agility the creatures display when dancing through the tree tops.

Speaking of tree tops, Sugar Gliders are arboreal, meaning that they spend the majority of their lives in the trees. They aren't picky about what type of forest they live in- indeed, their range encompasses a variety of forest types (from the ever wet rain forests of New Guinea to the drier woodlands of temperate Australia)- but they do seem to prefer to nesting in larger old trees with hollows. They are opportunist omnivores, meaning they can eat a wide variety of plant and animal life to sustain them. Of course, they are best known for their voracious appetite for sweet tree sap, hence their name. In fact, they will use their incisor teeth to scrape at the bark of trees to access said sap, their preferred food.

In terms of family arrangements, wild sugar gliders always live in groups. Usually such groups have at least 7 members, although more is not uncommon. There is a lead male, who marks both members of his group, and his territory using his scent marking glands (located in the head and chest). Those without the markings will be fought off.

Sugar gliders and humans
The indigenous aborigines of Australia used Sugar Gliders not for companionship, but rather as a source of food and fur. Native hunters

would look for tree hollows with scratch marks and patches of fur in their vicinity. Sugar Glider fur in particular was prized for use as armlets. However, not all aborigines used them for food and fur; some considered the Sugar Glider sacred and limited or prohibited hunting of the animal. In New Guinea, native shamans believed that witches would turn into Sugar Gliders in order to spy on their victims.

Modern history of the sugar glider
Although undoubtedly some aborigines must have kept individual Sugar Gliders as pets during the many thousands of years of overlap in their history in Australia, we first see mention of Sugar Gliders being kept as pets in colonial Australia in 1834. In a report to the Minutes of the Tasmanian Society in 1845, noted naturalist Ronald Campbell Gunn, FRS, had commented that marsupial gliders had become established in what is now known as Tasmania as early as 1834. He concluded that they were brought over by Australian settlers from the mainland as pets. The rest, as you can say, is history.

In more modern times, Sugar Gliders were first introduced to the United States in 1994, and have become wildly popular, with an estimated 1.1 million Sugar Gliders in captivity in the United States. It appears Sugar Gliders were imported into Great Britain around the same time as part of an increasing demand for exotic pets. Their popularity has exploded across the world in intervening years, with established breeders existing in places as far away as South Africa.

Responsible Ownership
With any pet, a good deal of research should be done before committing to ownership. This is all the more important with an exotic species, such as the Sugar Glider. Owing to the unique characteristic and life history of the species, special attention should be paid to your Sugar Gliders individual needs. This book will help demystify the more challenging aspects of Sugar Glider ownership.

Should I adopt or should I find a responsible breeder?
This is a question that is easiest to answer depending on your individual circumstances. Generally, in places with well-established Sugar Glider populations, such as many cities in the United States, there are Sugar Glider rescue organizations seeking to rehome Sugar Gliders (often time for free or very little money, relatively speaking). A quick internet search should let you know if such an organization exists near to you. If you want to hand select a Sugar Glider, or do not live near an area with a large Sugar Glider population, you may need to find a reputable breeder.

Adoption:
Pros
- Rescuing a Sugar Glider from its unfortunate circumstances
- Often cheaper than outright buying a Sugar Glider
- Networking opportunities with Sugar Glider rescuers

Cons
- Not knowing what circumstances your Sugar Glider has grown up in
- Not knowing the breeding history of your Sugar Glider
- Pre-existing medical issues

Finding a responsible breeder:
Pros
- Being able to hand select your Sugar Glider
- Knowing the full medical history of your Sugar Glider
- Knowing the breeding history of your Sugar Glider

Cons
- Usually much more expensive than adoption
- Be sure to do your due diligence in making sure your breeder is reputable. If not you may not get what you bargained for.

The choice between adopting or purchasing your Sugar Glider is entirely on you. Both choices have ethical aspects to them. With adopting, you're taking some burden of care off of some wonderful rescue organizations. With purchasing, you get to control all the variables of raising your Sugar Glider. Ultimately, you need to take time to reflect with yourself and discuss this issue with whomever in your family that would be impacted by bringing a Sugar Glider home.

Fast Facts

How long will my sugar glider live?
Sugar gliders, like most other animals, live longer in captivity. Sugar Gliders have a life expectancy of approximately 15 years. This demonstrates that with proper care, they can live long fulfilling lives as pets.

How much will my sugar glider cost?
While prices vary between breeders and appearance of the Sugar Glider, most Sugar Gliders seem to retail for between $250/£190 and $500/£380 each. Prices for rarer types can go much higher. Adoption fees have a wide range as well. Naturally you can find an owner on an online forum that

wishes to rehome a Sugar Glider at no cost to you (you might even get a free habitat/food out of it), or you can adopt directly from a rescue organization for a small donation.

Habitat costs

Habitats, much like the Sugar Gliders themselves, can be bought or "adopted". Entry level cages appear to cost about $100/£75, whereas higher end aviary-style cages can get to as high as $500/£380. Of course there are many wonderful custom built habitats as well, these cost as much as any custom habitat for an exotic pet would cost (generally, not cheap). Regardless of the budget, you must remember Sugar Gliders are social animals, meaning you must have adequate space for multiple Sugar Gliders, ideally.

Food costs

This is probably the aspect of Sugar Glider husbandry that costs the least. Although there are finer points about their nutrition that we will cover in later chapters, due to their size and preferred diet, it should cost approximately $10/£8 a month per sugar glider to feed adequately.

Veterinary costs

Assuming no emergencies or accidents, typical vet costs average out to $10/£8 a month- amongst the most affordable of any pet!

Chapter 2. Preparing for your Sugar Glider

This chapter will explain what ground work is necessary before you acquire your new Sugar Glider. The first step to proper ownership is to ask the right questions of yourself, the owner. Answer the questions in this chapter frankly and honestly, and you'll be able to better assess whether or not a Sugar Glider is the right pet for you at this time and place.

Is a Sugar Glider the right pet?

Of course Sugar Gliders are adorable- everyone loves to look at them and handle them. However, it is important to realize that admiring a Sugar Glider and owning a Sugar Glider are two entirely different things. Although hardly the most strenuous pets to own, they do have their unique challenges that may not line up with your lifestyle as well as you would think. Remember, once you have your Sugar Glider, it is entirely dependent on you for all aspects of its well-being.

Responsibilities

How have you handled other pets in the past? Have you become disenchanted with them after they have passed their "cute phase"? Have you gotten rid of any pets before because you have tired of them? If you have answered yes to any of the above, rest assured, you too will grow tired of your Sugar Glider(s). An ideal owner is a permanent owner, and there are already many Sugar Gliders at the mercy of rescue organizations in need of a home. Please think long and hard before making the commitment to become a responsible pet owner.

Making time for and bonding with your Sugar Glider

Understand that your Sugar Glider is <u>nocturnal</u>. This means that, by its very nature, it will be awake and active primarily during night time hours. Those cute bulging eyes are for helping it see in the dark, not for winning hearts over. If you are a natural night owl, then a Sugar Glider will probably jive with your natural schedule. If you are early to bed and early to rise, a Sugar Glider will probably be a tough addition to your life. *Ideally*, the Sugar Glider will be provided a quiet place during day time hours to sleep undisturbed.

Aside from the special scheduling considerations of owning a nocturnal pet, time must be devoted to developing a healthy bond with your Sugar Glider(s). The Sugar Glider will bond with its primary caregiver over all others (although they are social and can bond with others as well) due to their inherently hierarchical nature in the wild. Even a Sugar Glider adopted at an older age will bond with its caregiver, given enough time. Bonding with a Sugar Glider is not entirely unlike bonding with any other animal- you basically need to put in time to demonstrate to your Sugar Glider you are caring and kind, rather than some sort of hideous giant that tramps around the house during its sleeping hours.

Proper Bonding Techniques for your Sugar Glider
First off, many licensed breeder and rescue organizations will provide a plethora of information about bonding with your Sugar Glider. These people typically have years of experience handling Sugar Gliders at all stages of their life (from joey to adulthood), and will be more than happy to answer any specific concerns you may have about bonding with your Sugar Glider. Each Sugar Glider, like every person, has their own unique personality, so their bonding needs will be highly individualized. Always feel free to reach out to your breeder/rescue organization for help; they love Sugar Gliders as much as you do!

That being said, there are some general guidelines regarding bonding. Like with most animals, the best time to bond with a Sugar Glider is when it is still a joey (baby) - between 7 and 12 weeks out-of-pouch. Like a baby of any variety (human or otherwise) - the time invested in making your joey familiar with you will pay off handsomely. The more time, the better. Due to the gregarious nature of Sugar Gliders, if properly socialized from early on, much like dog puppies, they can bond with an entire family. Remember, in the wild, they live in groups, so there is no reason they can't become comfortable with your entire family group as well, given enough time and proper handling. And, yes, this can extend to other household pets as well, as long as you know those pets will not be inclined to eat your Sugar Glider!

A common technique to help the bonding process is to expose the Sugar Glider to your odor. There are several ways of going about this. One is simply to have the Sugar Glider on you as frequently as possible, including in your pockets or in a bonding purse you can carry with you. Another technique is simply taking a piece of cloth, and rubbing it all over you (and additional family members!) and putting it in their habitat for them to nest in. You may also drape an unwashed piece of laundry over their cage as well, as long as there is nothing they can unravel. Through exposure to these techniques, they will become more familiar with you and your family's smells.

An important note is that your new Sugar Glider is unfamiliar with you. It's the first time it has ever seen you, and you are hundreds of times larger than it is. It's going to react instinctively- that is- it's going to make a racket (they make a particular "crabbing" noise, which we will cover later in the book). They may even strike at you; that is, they'll pounce and nibble, usually after crabbing first. Remember, you are much larger than your Sugar Glider, no matter how ill willed it is, it can do you no real harm. You need to take charge (of course, in a gentle fashion, it's much smaller than you are) and stop being bossed around by your Sugar Glider.

If you happen to get a younger Sugar Glider, you can speed up the bonding process by putting it in a "starter" cage- that is, a smaller cage. Part of the reason is simply ease of access for you, the owner. You can just reach in there and handle him quickly, versus having to chase the Sugar Glider around a larger habitat. It's also *not* suggested you put a hanging fleece bag inside the starter cage. The baby Sugar Glider will love the pouch! That's not the problem. The problem is, the Sugar Glider is simply sleeping suspended in the air, and all of a sudden a large hand comes from seemingly nowhere to grab it. How would you react? The Sugar Glider will probably go into attack mode. This will *not* speed up bonding. A nesting cloth is far more appropriate, as it will have some cues ahead of time that you are coming (it'll feel the cage open, for example) and be familiar with the scent of the large hand coming in to grab it.

What time frame can you expect bonding to occur? Well, like any other animal, it varies. On a day to day basis, it's suggested you spend as much time as possible with your Sugar Glider. Of course it doesn't have to be all day everyday- although like a human baby, there is no such thing as "too much time" spent together, although there is such a thing as too little. As for the *process*, remember, bonding doesn't happen at any particular moment, it is a *process*. In rare cases, as little as in a few days. For some of the more hard headed joeys, a few months aren't unheard of either. It's a process that has some back and forth to it- the key to proper bonding is your persistence and investing the proper amount of time. You eventually came to love even the most annoying members of your family with enough time, the joey will too (assuming you are even annoying it).

Are they easy to potty train?

The answer is a qualified yes. If you think a Sugar Glider is like a cat, that can be trained to use a litter box, you are mistaken. Now, do not give up hope and surrender yourself to a home covered in Sugar Glider "treats", they are smart little animals and respond to conditioning (think of it as subconscious training). They have a routine more akin to that of a dog. Like dogs (or even human beings), they like to go to the bathroom when they first wake up. They have a pattern that you'll need to understand in order to successfully potty train your Sugar Glider. Also, potty training a Sugar Glider will take a little more equipment and a more hands on approach, than say, a puppy would.

First things first. You'll need to begin potty training as soon as you get your new Sugar Glider. They are creatures of habit, and this is definitely one habit you want to instil in your Sugar Glider. You will need newspaper and (unscented) baby wipes to properly potty train your Sugar Glider. Have them set up in front of the cage before you begin training, and keep this equipment close at hand until the entire training process has resulted in a potty trained Sugar Glider; this is not a 1 day process. The training procedure is done in three steps:

- Step 1- Over the newspaper; hold the Sugar Glider in one hand, with its back on your fingers and your thumb *gently* holding its belly. Make sure you have the right end of the Sugar Glider pointed towards the newspaper. If the Sugar Glider has not relieved itself after a few moments, gently wipe its bottom with the baby wipe. This will stimulate it to excrete urine and faeces.

- Step 2- Tubing. You need to make a tube shape with your free hand and let the Sugar Glider crawl through it. Generally, make the shape your hand would form as if you were holding and pulling in a rope. Take your other hand and form a tube shape as well, and let it crawl through there. This will stimulate your Sugar Glider to excrete whatever else it is storing. You *may* get some on you, but with practice, hopefully you'll be able to always have its rear end dangling when the moment comes. Do this for a period of time from a few seconds to a few minutes.

- Step 3- Repeat step one, except immediately rub the rear end with the baby wipe. This is simply to see if they have anything else left in them.

This whole procedure should take between 1 and 5 minutes. Do not rush them, or else they may not finish properly, which means they will finish at a time and place that is worse for you.

Recall that Sugar Gliders are nocturnal. We are diurnal (awake during daylight hours). When you are asleep, what is the most common reason for you to wake up? To go to the bathroom, of course! Sugar Gliders are no different from us in this respect. So if you happen to be walking around with your sugar glider, since you probably follow a daytime schedule, it will be asleep in your pocket. If you feel it wake up and stir, it's probably for the same reason you wake up in the middle of the night. Do the 3 steps as soon as you can over newspaper, and chances are the Sugar Glider will comfortably resume its slumber in your pocket shortly thereafter.

With enough time and maturation on your Sugar Glider's part (assuming you started potty training when it was still a joey, remember, babies are always prone to accidents); hopefully you can get your Sugar Glider to go to the bathroom pretty quickly. Potty training works just as well with adult Sugar Gliders, although it may take a little time as it's harder to change habits at an older age. You can tell potty training is complete when you can hold the Sugar Glider with your hand flat over the newspaper, gently lift its tail and it starts relieving itself quickly.

How do I choose the right Veterinarian or Breeder?

Now that you have familiarized yourself with the background and basic behaviors of Sugar Gliders, it comes to selection time. Before even beginning the search for your Sugar Glider, you will need to choose a veterinarian to take it to. Why so early? Well, when have you ever planned for a medical emergency? Luckily, for humans, there are well qualified doctors at every emergency room. For exotic species like Sugar Gliders, there are far fewer qualified professionals that deal with their health care. As for a breeder, it's important to select one that matches several suggested guidelines to make sure your Sugar Glider gets the best start in life as possible. Remember, with rescue agencies, you are essentially doing a charitable act- simply look for the 501(c)(3) designation if you are in the United States or search your Charity Commission's registry if in the United Kingdom to verify that the organization is indeed a bona fide charity.

Selecting a Veterinarian
A Sugar Glider is a small *exotic* marsupial pet native to the Australasia region. The operative word being "exotic"- this means you should, ideally, search for a veterinarian that specializes in exotic species. Although Sugar Gliders have become more main stream in recent years, they are not yet

well established enough to guarantee your everyday veterinarian will be intimately familiar with all the most up to date guidelines for proper Sugar Glider care, diagnosis, treatment and procedures. Think of how many people you know have Sugar Gliders? I bet you the number isn't as high as the number of people you know that have dogs or cats, now is it? Another good reason for seeking out an exotic animal veterinarian instead of a regular veterinarian for your Sugar Glider is in case your Sugar Glider should ever need a specialized treatment or surgical procedure.

If your Sugar Glider needs emergency treatment, it would be nice to have its entire medical history in one clinic, rather than having to wait for all the relevant case history and files to be transferred between practices. With the internet at hand, it shouldn't be too difficult to find an exotic animal veterinarian with plenty of reviews from which to make an informed choice.

Selecting a breeder
Since Sugar Gliders are an exotic species (presuming you're not reading this from Australia), special care must go into where you source your Sugar Glider from. In the United States, it is preferred you buy from a breeder with an up to date USDA license. Sugar Gliders are a regulated species in the United States under the jurisdiction of the USDA (United States Department of Agriculture). Some jurisdictions in the United States have even begun requiring owners to prove they sourced their Sugar Gliders from a USDA licensed breeder.

This ensures your Sugar Glider has met, at the very least, the minimum requirement for health and sanitation when it was bred. The Animal Welfare Act does exempt Sugar Glider breeders who have only four or fewer females and gross less than $500 a year from selling offspring from having a license. For the United Kingdom, there doesn't seem to be a corresponding license requirement for the breeding of Sugar Gliders.

Instead, follow advice that would apply anywhere else. It's always preferable to see your breeder in person, to make sure the conditions the Sugar Glider was bred are in fact humane and sanitary. Of course, small time breeders may not feel compelled to let you into their homes, which is fine. Ask for photo and video documentation of both the Sugar Gliders in question (joey and the parents) and their conditions. You may want to word the question in such a way that you're asking a clearer idea of what is an acceptable set up. A proud Sugar Glider breeder should have no problems proving they are raising them in humane conditions. Ask them what the parents' diets are, how long have they been involved with Sugar Gliders, etc. This should help solidify your confidence that you are in fact dealing with competent experienced Sugar Glider breeders.

If, for whatever reason, you need to have your Sugar Gliders shipped to you, make sure the courier they choose has experience in shipping live animals (a DEFRA licensed courier in the United Kingdom) and that the animals are shipped same day/overnight in climate controlled conditions. No reputable breeder would object to any of these conditions. Indeed, it is a little more expensive than shipping a television or a table for example, but what price can you really put to ensure your Sugar Glider arrives in healthy condition?

Must Have's - What to buy

The list of requirements in order to adequately house and care for a Sugar Glider is as follows:

- A starter cage (if purchasing a joey)
- An adult habitat (an aviary style cage, at least 24" x 24" x 48", 60cm x 60cm x 121cm)
- Lining paper (you don't really think you'll be awake in the middle of the night to help your Sugar Glider go to the bathroom each time, do you?)
- Unscented baby wipes (this helps with potty training, as discussed earlier)
- A Sugar Glider wheel (for exercise)
- A pouch or cube to sleep in (you may want to wait until you are bonded with your Sugar Glider for this purchase)
- Nail file (not a clipper!)
- Food
- Water dispenser

You should consider the above list minimum criteria to adequately care for your Sugar Glider. There is a wide variety of other accessories and toys you may consider purchasing for your sugar glider in order to enrich their environment, but this is at your discretion.

Lone male, lone female, a pair or multiple sugar gliders?

Sugar Gliders are social animals!
It can never be suggested in good consciousness that you buy a lone Sugar Glider. Indeed, Sugar Gliders are used as a model animal in psychology labs for their social behavior; their colonies are so complex socially that colony hierarchal manipulation (and the loss of social status) is used as an

analogue for human depression. As discussed earlier in the natural history section of this book, Sugar Gliders are always found living in groups in the wild. Human beings live in social groups, and become distressed if isolated for long periods of time due to their social nature. The same goes for Sugar Gliders. At a minimum, you should always have 2 Sugar Gliders, although more is considered merrier. That being said, the gender makeup of the colony is up to you. Some example of stable colony population set ups:

- All neutered males
- All spayed females and neutered males
- All females
- All male colony (if raised together)

Note that it is NOT suggested to have fertile pairings together unless you want them to breed. Unless you are ready for a far bigger commitment and have a homing plan in mind, it is suggested in the strongest terms possible to please *not* breed your Sugar Gliders! There are enough unwanted and under cared for Sugar Gliders in the world as is!

Legal issues

It is imperative that you check your local laws regarding ownership of Sugar Gliders. While they may not have as many restrictions on them as say a tiger, most jurisdictions still consider them to be exotic pets. They range from perfectly legal, requiring no paperwork, to absolutely prohibited with no exceptions for private ownership. We will try to cover as many jurisdictions as possible below, but please be aware that legislation is consistently changing, and that at the time of publication for this book, your local laws may very well have changed.

Legality in the United States (state by state)

Alabama : Legal with no apparent restrictions.

Alaska : Illegal without exception for private ownership. Alaska has a very strict list of what animals may and may not be kept as pets. Through omission on the permitted pet list, Sugar Gliders are banned. (Statute 5 AAC 92.029. Permit for possessing live game).

Arizona : Legal with no apparent restrictions.

Arkansas : Legal with no apparent restrictions.

California : California has very strict laws as to what species fall under the category of suitable pets. All marsupials are explicitly prohibited for private ownership. [Importation, Transportation and Possession of Live Restricted Animals, 14 CCR § 671. (2)(C)].

Colorado : Legal with no apparent restrictions.

Connecticut : Legal with no apparent restrictions.

Delaware : Legal with no apparent restrictions.

Florida : Legal to own, but there are mandated guidelines for the conditions they may be kept in.

Georgia : Legal, as long as you can produce documentation that you purchased your Sugar Glider through a USDA licensed breeder.

Hawaii : Due to ecological catastrophes in the past caused by exotic species introduction, Hawaii has some of the strictest laws in the nation on pet ownership. There appears to be an absolute prohibition on the possession of Sugar Gliders in Hawaii.

Idaho : Legal without restrictions.

Illinois : Legal without restrictions.

Indiana : Legal without restrictions.

Iowa : Legal without restrictions.

Kansas : Legal without restrictions.

Kentucky : Legal without restrictions.

Louisiana : Legal without restrictions.

Maine : Legal, but there may be restrictions when it comes to breeding, as they would be considered under the broad scope of "small mammals".

Maryland : Legal to own, although a license is needed to sell Sugar Gliders.

Massachusetts : Legal to own without any permitting. The legalization happened relatively recently (in 2014), so many websites still say they are prohibited. This is no longer the case.

Michigan : Legal to own without restrictions.

Minnesota : Legal to own without restrictions.

Mississippi : Legal to own without restrictions.

Missouri : Legal to own without restrictions.

Montana : Legal to own without restrictions.

Nebraska : Legal to own without restrictions.

Nevada : Legal to own without restrictions.

New Hampshire : Legal to own without restrictions.

New Jersey : New Jersey has somewhat restrictive pet laws. They maintain a list of exotic species that are you are allowed to own without a permit. Sugar Gliders are *not* on that list, therefore, you will need a permit to legally possess a Sugar Glider.

New Mexico : According to the New Mexico Game and Fish Director's Species Importation List, Sugar Gliders are a Group II species meaning they are "live non-domesticated animals that are not known to be either invasive or dangerous and do not present a known risk to the health, safety or well-being of the public, domestic livestock or to native wildlife and their habitats.". You will need to apply for a permit in order to legally obtain or own a Sugar Glider.

New York : They are legal in most of the state, but explicitly illegal in New York City.

North Carolina : Legal without restrictions.

North Dakota : Legal without restrictions.

Ohio : Legal without restrictions.

Oklahoma : Legal without restrictions.

Oregon : Legal without restrictions.

Pennsylvania : You will need to apply for a permit in order to get a Sugar Glider. Since the permit is subject to commission review, it's probably pretty difficult to get approval.

Rhode Island : Legal without restrictions.

South Carolina : Legal without restrictions.

South Dakota : Legal without restrictions.

Tennessee : Legal without restrictions.

Texas : Legal without restrictions.

Utah : Legal with permit restrictions.

Vermont : Legal without restrictions.

Virginia : Legal without restrictions.

Washington : Legal without restrictions.

West Virginia : Legal without restrictions.

Wisconsin : Legal without restrictions.

Wyoming : Legal without restrictions.

Legality in the United Kingdom
At the time of writing, there appears to be no restrictions to Sugar Glider ownership within the United Kingdom. It never hurts to check with your local council to be sure of this fact.

Legality in Canada
The legality of Sugar Gliders is highly variable, with local government's often prohibiting ownership of Sugar Gliders. There are no Province-wide bans on the ownership of Sugar Gliders, although many municipalities do prohibit or otherwise place restrictions on ownership of Sugar Gliders. Ontario in particular appears to have the most municipalities with prohibitions and restrictions on Sugar Gliders. To provide an exhaustive list of municipalities that restrict or outright ban Sugar Gliders in Canada

would appear to fill a volume of books, so it is suggested that you simply check in with your local authorities to see if they are permitted.

Legality in Australia/New Zealand

Due to Sugar Gliders in fact being indigenous to Australia, there are many restrictions on their ownership. In fact, the export of Sugar Gliders from Australia has been prohibited for many years.

New South Wales : Ownership of Sugar Gliders is not permitted.

Victoria : You need a private wildlife license in order to keep a Sugar Glider.

South Australia : Sugar Gliders are listed as a "basic" native species, meaning that they are very common in their natural habitat and that no permit is required to own a single member of the species. A permit is required to sell members of the species, however.

Western Australia : Private ownership of Sugar Gliders is forbidden, only zoological facilities may possess them.

Australian Capital Territory : They are permitted as pets.

Tasmania : Sugar Gliders are not permitted as pets, as they are considered protected wildlife under legislation passed in 2010. One could apply for a wildlife rehabilitation permit to nurse injured wild Sugar Gliders back to good health, but this does not permit long term ownership of any wild Sugar Gliders.

Queensland : The only way to legally obtain and own a Sugar Glider is to hold a demonstrators permit. You would need to keep records of making public educational demonstrations with the Sugar Glider at least once a month. This is not what most people have in mind when they have a pet, so in reality, Sugar Gliders are all but banned for private non-institutional ownership in Queensland.

Northern Territory : Sugar Gliders are permitted as pets. The only restrictions are that you buy your Sugar Glider from a registered seller, keep the receipt and submit a copy of the receipt along with your application to keep wildlife.

Chapter 3. Coming Home

So you have made the decision to bring a Sugar Glider home, after checking and researching. It has been a process, no doubt. You had to exam your motives for ownership, make sure your lifestyle is congruent with Sugar Glider ownership, find a reputable breeder or rescue agency and check your local laws to make sure ownership is even legal. You are almost ready to bring your Sugar Glider home. There is just one last question- where do you put it?

Site selection for the habitat

Site selection for the Sugar Gliders habitat usually has some nuance, and every home is different. One universal concern about Sugar Glider cage placement though is noise. Remember that Sugar Gliders are primarily nocturnal animals. If you are a night owl (or an incredibly deep sleeper) and don't mind hearing Sugar Glider activities all night, then by all means, put the cage in your bedroom if you would like. Most people, however, prefer to keep their Sugar Glider cages in a common area, so that the normal habits of the Sugar Glider don't disturb their sleep.

There are also safety concerns about where you should put your Sugar Glider cage. Please don't put your cage somewhere where it will be exposed to direct sunlight during the day. First of all, Sugar Gliders are nocturnal, so they are not the biggest fans of sunlight to begin with. It is hard enough for you to sleep with a spotlight in your face, imagine the poor Sugar Glider! More pressing, however, is that they may overheat when you are not paying attention- they are far smaller creatures than you are and are more sensitive to temperature extremes for this reason.

Basically, think of a place in your home you would be comfortable sitting at for a few hours straight- not too much light, not too much heat. Sugar Gliders are most comfortable at a temperature of 75 (23 C) to 80 degrees (27 C). This is probably the best spot for your Sugar Glider cage.

A word of warning. The two most dangerous rooms in your home for a Sugar Glider are the bathroom and the kitchen. The bathroom has a little feature called the toilet. Although dogs and cats may drink out of the bowl with little to no harm (yuck!), if a Sugar Glider should fall into the bowl and escape your notice for a few minutes, it may very well drown. It has happened to other owners before. Although putting your Sugar Glider cage in the bathroom is a little odd, and most wouldn't do it, for the toilet reason alone, it is not suggested in the first place. The kitchen has more subtle reasons for posing a serious danger to your Sugar Glider. Yes, there are sharp objects there, and most people would not want to keep an animal enclosure where they cook food anyway. However, food cooking is exactly the most dangerous part of your kitchen for your Sugar Glider.

First of all, many foods we can eat, the Sugar Glider cannot- we will cover this in more detail later on in the book. If your Sugar Glider should eat something without you noticing because someone threw it into its cage during food preparation, or you allow it free reign in the kitchen, it could end badly. More subtly, fumes pose a real danger to your Sugar Glider. In particular, fumes given off by nonstick cookware are lethal to most small animals, and food fumes probably aren't the best thing for your Sugar Glider anyways; imagine if you knew someone was lethally allergic to certain foods, would you cook that food around them?

Making sure your Sugar Glider settles in

As a responsible pet owner, you have a duty to ensure your Sugar Glider has a comfortable life. As with most things, first impressions matter, so start off your relationship with your Sugar Glider on the right foot. Please make sure you have an appropriate habitat (the details of which we will cover later in this book) and food awaiting your Sugar Glider during its first few days in its new home. Have the habitat set up in an appropriate spot- your Sugar Glider has already had to endure one big move, another big move will only stress it out further.

Most importantly, consider the age of your Sugar Glider and the age appropriate bonding requirements for your Sugar Glider. Your Sugar Glider is not a house plant, and will require human interaction to become an ideal pet. Make sure you have easy access to it, and that you will follow the age appropriate bonding procedures we discussed in earlier chapters.

Chapter 4. Day to day life with your Sugar Glider

Life with your Sugar Glider needs to take on certain rhythms. Just as one would have a schedule for walking the dog, or feeding the cat, your Sugar Glider should become a part of your daily routine. The more time you spend with your Sugar Glider, the more rewarding of a pet you will have. Sugar Gliders are not quite like cats or dogs, but with a little adjustment and planning, they can fit nicely into your schedule.

Making a comfortable schedule

For about the millionth time, Sugar Gliders are nocturnal! This means they are naturally inclined to be more active at night than during day. Some may ask "Can I keep them in a dark room all day and keep them in a lit room all night to reverse their natural schedule?"- to which the answer is, only if you have a veterinary or zoological degree. It sounds good in theory, but this is an extremely difficult thing to actually carry out in person. If you mess with their schedule and don't stick to the adjusted schedule perfectly, you can seriously stress your Sugar Glider. Think about how bad it would feel to have your day/night cycle reversed, even once without advance notice? You are only human, and are bound to forget to sticking to such a rigid regimen.

The better route is to work with your Sugar Gliders natural schedule. There is a natural overlap in human diurnal (day time loving) and Sugar Gliders nocturnal schedule- that is, in the evenings and mornings. Just as you don't fall asleep as soon as the sky turns dark, your Sugar Glider won't fall asleep as soon as it spots a little bit of dawn light. Technically, this means you and your Sugar Glider will ideally have a crepuscular interaction time (that is, in the evenings and mornings) schedule.

For most people, mornings are a little tight schedule wise, with jobs and schools and all. All the better, your Sugar Glider is no doubt starting to wind down from a long night. This means most Sugar Glider owners will interact with their furry companion after the work day, in the early evening. This doesn't mean you shouldn't ever interact with your Sugar Glider during daylight hours (especially when bonding and trying to house break your pet), but keep it to a somewhat minimum. You would be quite cranky if people consistently woke you up in the middle of the night.

Finding a lost Sugar Glider

Sugar Gliders can be quite the escape artists- they are small, fast and agile, so you really need to keep an eye on where they are at all times. That being said, from time to time, your Sugar Glider will get lost, that is just a fact of life for Sugar Glider owners. Most of the time, if it has only been a few minutes in a familiar setting, just look in the regular spots you would find your Sugar Glider. However, with more serious cases of missing Sugar Gliders, there are certain protocols.

What to do if your Sugar Glider is lost indoors

If you are absolutely certain your Sugar Glider is hidden away somewhere in your house, the best approach is to practice a little silent patience. First things first, go around and close any lids to any bodies of water in your home (toilet lid, fish tank lid, etc.) to make sure your curious Sugar Glider does not drown exploring. It is also a good idea to close up any sort of holes or vents they may want to explore (and of course, check in them to make sure your Sugar Glider is not already in there). Once these hazards have been accounted for, it is on to the next step.

If you have done a casual search of your home and the Sugar Glider has not turned up, there is a good chance it is asleep somewhere, sleepily ignoring your pleas. This is especially true during daylight hours. Your best bet is to have something to entice it when it wakes up. Take your Sugar Glider cage, open the door, and leave it in the general vicinity of where you last saw your Sugar Glider (or where you suspect it is currently hiding). Put your Sugar Gliders favorite treats in and on the cage- with a bit of luck, when it wakes up, it will head straight for the cage. Vigilance is important, so check on the cage every few minutes to see if your rogue Sugar Glider has turned up.

If your Sugar Glider has not been found after these few steps, it is time to practice the silence and patience I urged earlier. Wait until the evening, turn off all the lights in the house, and listen closely. Wait in hand with a flashlight. Your Sugar Glider is a noisy creature, and once it gets its night going, it will make a quite a few sounds. When you think you have spotted him, turn the flashlight on in its direction- this will startle your Sugar Glider (the term is called spotlighting) for a few moments. Use this time to your advantage to grab the Sugar Glider and put it back into the safety of its cage.

What to do if your Sugar Glider is lost outdoors

First things first. You should never take your Sugar Glider outdoors when it is not in its cage! Your Sugar Glider is soft, and furry and moves like an adorable little critter. To you it is cute, to a predator, it looks like supper. You may think you are safe if the Sugar Glider is on you, but you are not. Like all other pets, your Sugar Glider has a mind of its own. If it sees something interesting or just gets tired of hanging on you, it will jump away from you. Even if it does stay on you, this does not rule out possible attack from other animals. Young dogs and cats in particular may try to snatch the Sugar Glider off of you. Even if you know for a fact there are no dogs or cats in your yard, you cannot be so certain about birds of prey. There are plenty of heart breaking videos on the internet where an owner of a small mammal walks out into their yard with pet in hand only to have it snatched by an owl or hawk before they can react. You have been warned!

If *somehow* your Sugar Glider has escaped to the great outdoors, your options are somewhat more limited than indoors. Follow as many applicable safety protocols as possible (instead of closing toilet bowls, cover buckets of water, drinking troughs, etc.) on your property. Place your Sugar Glider cage outdoors, door open with a variety of treats. After searching, all you can do at this point is wait. Odds are actually very good your Sugar Glider will come home- it knows where its bread is buttered. If it still has not returned to the cage, mount a night search with your flashlight. The more people involved, the merrier.

Just remember silence is important, since you are far more likely to hear your Sugar Glider than see it (it being so small and grey to brown colored). Once you think you have located it, turn the flashlight on and startle it. Using a pillowcase may increase your odds of capturing any particularly rebellious Sugar Gliders. Once you have captured your Sugar Glider, please take the time to review any mistakes you may have made that led to its initial escape (whether indoors or outdoors). The world at large is rather dangerous for your Sugar Glider, and the fact that you have found it again is a second chance with your pet. There is the saying that an ounce of prevention is worth a pound of cure.

Traveling with your sugar glider

Good news! Your Sugar Glider is quite portable! Just follow a few safety precautions and you can travel quite easily with your Sugar Glider. Please understand that it is important to understand your Sugar Gliders habits to make the process of traveling as comfortable as possible for you and your pet.

Where are you taking your Sugar Glider?
This is the most important question to ask! Truly think of where you are going with your pet. You may be tempted to take it everywhere with you, but remember, it is a fragile animal. It is natural to want to show it off to a few friends, but perhaps taking your Sugar Glider to a house party, for example, is not the best idea. Will there be factors in the environment that make the place aggravating or even dangerous for your Sugar Glider? Loud noises, crowds of people, other pets, escape opportunities, etc. all have to be considered in advance.

Everyday Traveling with your Sugar Glider
If you want your Sugar Glider to go with you to everyday places, please make sure you are well bonded to the Sugar Glider. A pet that does not want to be around you will take its first opportunity to escape. That being said, most of the time, your Sugar Glider can ride around with you in your pocket. Yes, it is that simple. Most of the time, you will be traveling around during daylight hours, and since your pocket is a pretty close analogue to a pouch, your Sugar Glider will happily sleep in your pocket while you go about your business.

Of course, keep your Sugar Gliders bathroom supplies near at hand- chances are if it is waking during daylight hours, it needs to go to the bathroom! Naturally, be *very* aware of where your Sugar Glider is sleeping on you so you don't squash it when you are sitting!

If you are traveling when the Sugar Glider is most likely to be active (like night time), take extra precautions. For those portions of the trip that are not indoors, please make sure to travel with your Sugar Glider in a pet carrier. You really do not want to have to search for your Sugar Glider at night in a place you are not familiar with. If you are familiar with your destination, and it is indoors, it is OK to let the Sugar Glider cling onto you. If it gets uncomfortable, it will probably retreat into one of your pockets. Although leashes and harnesses are sold for Sugar Gliders, it is strongly suggested you do not use one.

Remember that Sugar Gliders have flaps (actually called a patagium), and if they should, for whatever reason, want to glide off of you and they have a leash on, they could damage this sensitive structure. Just learn to read your Sugar Gliders body language, and keep it as comfortable as possible at all times.

More Serious Traveling with your Sugar Glider

What you need to bring with you is determined by the length of your trip. The most basic accessory you will need will be your travel carrier. They do sell specialized Sugar Glider carriers that do work wonderfully, but many owners have simply taken cat carry crates and retrofitted them with a fine mesh on the door to keep their Sugar Glider from escaping. Whichever route you choose, just be sure your Sugar Glider cannot escape. Within your carrier, you should have some Sugar Glider pouches and soft bedding material. The bedding material does not necessarily have to be made for being soiled, it can simply be an old towel if it is shorter trip (like, say, to the veterinarians office). For a longer trip, one where you are checking them in on a flight, for example, you may want to go with the disposable bedding route.

Aside from the carrier, you will need to bring along food and water. Depending on the length of your journey, you may want to have a little case with several days' worth of Sugar Glider food, as it may not be the easiest thing to go out of your way to buy during a trip. Who goes on vacation and thinks "where am I going to buy mealworms?". Also, it's suggested you attach a waterer to your carrier. This way, whenever your Sugar Glider gets thirsty, it will have access to water.

If you should be traveling across states, provinces or countries it is essential you look into the legality of transporting your pet Sugar Glider across such borders. Just like a cat or dog, your Sugar Glider may need documentation proving its good health. It may also be subject to quarantine. The Sugar Glider may very well be banned from the jurisdiction you are are traveling to! It would be heart breaking to have your pet potentially seized and impounded during a vacation.

Please check with the local law enforcement at your intended destination to discuss the matter- they will be able to point you in the right direction. Usually it is either no problem at all, you need to provide paperwork, or an outright ban. These are all fine as long as you know in advance!

Chapter 5. Making a comfortable habitat for your sugar glider

Sugar Gliders, like any other pet, are going to need a home. As we spoke about earlier in the book, Sugar Gliders are going to need one of two types of set up. The first kind of set up is for young Sugar Gliders, or Sugar Gliders who need to learn how to bond with their owner (you see, not all unbonded Sugar Gliders are young, but all young Sugar Gliders are unbonded). The second type of set up is for bonded, more mature Sugar Gliders, their final habitat. It is more than just selecting a cage and throwing the critter in there.

General guidelines for choosing a cage

Bonding Cage
Please take a moment to review the bonding section of this book before selecting your cage. The gist of the bonding cage is to allow you to easily access your unbonded Sugar Glider quickly. If you are trying to make the animal accustomed to you, there is no point in chasing it around a large cage. In fact, the more prolonged the chase, the more distressed your animal will be. The bonding cage is *not* an appropriate long term home for your Sugar Glider. It should only be used for bonding purposes and once you and your Sugar Glider have established a trusting relationship, you should immediately move it into its permanent larger enclosure.

Permanent Cage
The rule of thumb for the cage is to buy the largest cage you can afford and keep comfortably in your home. There is no upper limit to how much space Sugar Gliders can use; remember, in the wild they are used to bouncing from tree to tree! Wouldn't you like more space in your life? Also, since you will most likely be having multiple Sugar Gliders, the bigger the space, the less friction between your pets.

The nitty gritty of what your cage should look like is important as well. If you have younger Sugar Gliders, it is suggested that you buy a Sugar Glider cage with PVC coating. This is because young Sugar Gliders (and joeys) have more delicate bone structure. The PVC coating will allow them to really sink their claws into the exterior of their cage and prevent slipping. Slipping a good distance down at a quick pace is a good way for your young Sugar Glider to break a bone! For this reason, you cannot just stick your Sugar Gliders into a regular old bird cage. The holes of the cage should be rectangular, and approximately 1 inch (2.5 cm) by ½ inch (1.2 cm). This should be small enough to keep most young Sugar Gliders and joeys in their enclosure securely.

When a Sugar Glider gets to about 4 or 6 months of age, it can handle a full sized cage. You must take into consideration the coating on the bars and the size of the gaps on the bars. The bar spacing must not exceed ½ inch (1.2 cm), or the Sugar Glider will probably be able to escape. They are quite like other small mammals in that they can scrunch themselves into small spaces to escape. The doors of your cage must also have safety latches, because unlike other small mammals, their paws are actually quite like little hands. They can manipulate objects pretty easily with their "hands", so a door with a safety latch should keep them from escaping that way.

You should also seriously consider going in person to buy your Sugar Glider cage. It is very difficult to guarantee the quality of your Sugar Glider cage online, especially when it comes to the coating of your Sugar Glider cage. You do not want a cage that has low quality coating (paint, etc.) that can flake off. The raw metal bars will expose your Sugar Gliders to excess zinc, and they may die from it. Always look for sturdy PVC plastic coating, never settle for paint! Luckily a Sugar Glider cage is a one off purchase, so do not cut corners on this aspect of raising your Sugar Glider.

Sugar Gliders come from a warm climate. Chances are very good you either do not live in a warm climate, or if you do, you set your air conditioning to a temperature that is comfortable for you. If you are comfortable at 75 to 80 degrees Fahrenheit (23 C to 27 C), then your Sugar Glider will also be comfortable. If your home is cooler than this, it is suggested you buy a heat rock or two, to supplement your Sugar Glider's habitat with a heat source. Your heat rock is perfectly safe for your Sugar Glider, indeed it was designed with far more fragile fauna in mind (reptiles in particular). If your Sugar Glider should become uncomfortable with it, assuming you have a decent sized cage, it will simply retreat from it. No worries.

Bedding, AKA the "poop tray"

Let's be honest. You are not going to be around 100% of the time for every single moment of your Sugar Gliders life. Inevitably, this means they are going to go to the bathroom when not in your presence. If you have not already, I urge you to go to the potty training section of this book to better understand your Sugar Gliders bathroom needs. Remember that Sugar Gliders, like most other small mammals cannot be reliably trained to defecate and urinate in a predetermined spot like a cat or dog. That being said, what do you do need to have set up when you are not around to help your Sugar Glider go to the bathroom?

You need to have reliable bedding in the bottom of your cage! Good news, if you wanted a cheap solution, most owners agree that non-toxic paper is suitable for the bottom of your cage. This includes newspapers, paper towels, etc. Of course there are custom designed cage liners for Sugar Gliders, and most of them are fantastic, but they may be pricier than regular old newspaper. Some people also use a towel or piece of velvet that they rewash periodically. Sugar Gliders being generally hygienic little animals do not produce a ton of waste, so if you are comfortable being a little more hands on, this might be the right approach for you as well. That being said, are there types of bedding that should not be used for Sugar Gliders?

Yes! Most veterinarians agree that wood shavings are not suitable as cage bedding for Sugar Gliders. In particular, pine or cedar shavings are especially dangerous for Sugar Gliders. That is because these wood shavings release an aromatic organic compound call phenols, which have been linked to kidney and liver damage in Sugar Gliders. Eventually, these compounds may kill your Sugar Glider, if they are left exposed to it for too long.

Where and how the sugar glider will sleep

Please read the section on where to put your cage first before reading this section. Where you place your cage will have far more impact on your Sugar Glider (and your own!) sleep than just however you arrange the sleeping items of your Sugar Gliders cage. That being said, there are some guidelines for setting up your cage to ensure your Sugar Glider gets a solid day's sleep.

Again, reiterating, your Sugar Glider is nocturnal. Besides health and safety reasons, you should never have your Sugar Glider in direct sunlight. They are sensitive to bright light, and no pouch or box is sufficiently opaque or cool enough to block out direct sunlight or its heat. Keep the cage in a common area and at the very least, in indirect sunlight. It is not suggested you keep your Sugar Glider in perfect darkness though. Remember, day time lighting is their cue to go to sleep, just as night time darkness is our cue to sleep. They have an internal biological rhythm for sleep patterns just like we do, and 24 hour darkness is just as unhealthy for them as 24 hour light would be for us.

There are two accessories in particular you should put in to your Sugar Glider cage to ensure a proper healthy sleep for your pet. The most universally accepted and popular sleep time accessory is the pouch. They are sold all over the place and come in a wide variety of patterns. If you are the arts and craft variety, you may feel inclined to make your own. Basically, you should be looking for a few features before deciding on what pouch you should buy.

It is suggested that the pouch should be able to hang vertically (that is, from the top of the cage), Sugar Gliders do seem to have a preference for this style of pouch. Perhaps it is because they don't like to feel a cage wall at their back? We'll only ever know if we ask the Sugar Gliders! Secondly, make sure your pouch is built well- loose threads are a hazard for Sugar Gliders (they may get wrapped up in it or ingest the thread). Thirdly, make sure your pouch is easy to clean. Accidents are most frequent inside these pouches.

The second most popular option is providing a nesting box for your Sugar Glider. Depending on your Sugar Glider, it may spend more time in here than a pouch (a pouch probably reminds it of its mothers pouch, where as a nesting box more resembles the tree hollows Sugar Gliders occupy in their natural habitats, every Sugar Glider is different in their tastes). People have used wooden birdhouses (as long as they avoid pine or cedar for the reasons covered in the bedding section), small mammal houses, etc. Ideally, your nesting box should have a removable or hinged lid to allow access to your Sugar Glider. Unlike a pouch, you can't fit your hand into or easily remove a Sugar Glider otherwise!

The opening for your Sugar Glider box should be 1.5 inches (3.8 cm) in diameter at the smallest. The reason for this minimum size is if you happen to have a female Sugar Glider with joeys clinging to her, she will find it difficult to climb in and out of a box with a hole smaller than this.

Also, resist the temptation to put the entrance to the nesting box square in the middle of the box. Instead, put it high on the box, so that parent Sugar Gliders can easily come in and out, but joeys won't fall out. The nesting box itself should be at least 6 x 6 inches (13 x 13 cm), and the nesting box bedding should consist of soft particular matter (soft paper, etc). For reasons explained earlier, you should avoid pine and cedar wood shavings within the nesting boxes themselves as well.

Heating and lighting

As stated earlier in the *Permanent Cage* section of the book, Sugar Gliders prefer things to be a little on the warmer side. You should ideally have an additional heat source in your cage to keep your Sugar Glider warm. The ideal temperature range is 75 to 80 degrees Fahrenheit (23 C to 27 C), consider using a heating rock or two to allow for a warm retreat for your Sugar Glider. Do *not* put the heat rock in the bedding or in a nesting box, as something may catch fire. As Sugar Gliders are nocturnal, they will not need any additional source of light in their enclosure. Direct sunlight exposure should be avoided, as it may damage their sensitive eyes.

Accessories

There are a plethora of toys and accessories you can buy for your Sugar Glider. A good rule of thumb is the more stimulation a pet has, the better its lifestyle, so don't skimp here. A word of warning however. Many, many small mammal toys have bells (or other sorts of noise makers) attached to them- it would best for you to remove them as soon as you buy the toy. Sugar Gliders will be most physically active at night, and this will be the time the bells or other noise makers will be most active as well!

The most important toy to purchase for your Sugar Glider is an exercise wheel. Aside from the cage itself, this is the single item that will require the most time and money on your part to adequately equip your Sugar Glider habitat.

You will need a larger Sugar Glider exercise wheel because they like to do hopping motions during running (as they would in the wild), and, due to the gregarious nature of Sugar Gliders, you will sometimes have multiple Sugar Gliders monkeying around in the wheel. Therefore, the minimum size of your exercise wheel should be about 18 inches in diameter (45 cm). You should also probably look specifically for Sugar Glider exercise wheels, as other wheels may not be up to par for having your Sugar Glider on.

First of all, cheaper exercise wheels may be noisy- again, your Sugar Glider will be most active when most people in your home will be asleep. Also, you need to be considerate of the Sugar Gliders large fluffy tail. Make sure your exercise wheel is meshed and does *not* have just crossbars- the tail may very well get stuck in there, and, in some extreme cases, get ripped off! Some owners also put trim tracks into their meshed exercise wheels (basically, sandpaper strips) to keep the Sugar Gliders claws maintained, this is fine. Please be sure to clean your exercise wheel every day, as they will defecate and urinate in it. If you allow urine and feces to accumulate, it will damage your exercise wheel.

For feeding and watering, the common accessories are fine for full grown Sugar Gliders. You may want to buy a glass pet water bottle for ease of sanitation- you do have to clean them out periodically. For very young joeys, you may need to have an open faced source of water just for them near their food- some have even suggested a bottle cap for water. Just make sure the water source isn't so large that there is a drowning risk. As for a feeding station- anything will do really.

They do sell higher end no mess stations, but regular old feeding trays, platers, etcetera will do. There are disposable and easily washable options as well.

Housing multiple sugar gliders together

Sugar Gliders are socially gregarious animals and need to live, at the minimum, in pairs. A group is even better. Consensus amongst owners and veterinarians is that for a pair of Sugar Gliders, the minimum cage space should be 36 inches (90 cm) tall by 18 inches deep (45 cm) by 30 inches wide (76 cm). This works out to 19,440 cubic inches (49,377 cm^3) for the pair, or approximately 9,700 cubic inches (24,600 cm^3) per Sugar Glider at a *minimum.*

Remember, bigger is always better, since these animals do travel relatively large distances in their natural habitat. As a human being, you have the ability to get out of the house, go to the mall, travel to various places- pet Sugar Gliders do not (at their own discretion, at least)! You would get cabin fever living in the minimal ethical living space for you and your family, but a home with a place for privacy will do much to allay your stress. It is the same thing with Sugar Gliders.

As for nesting boxes and pouches, the more the merrier as well. You may have noticed other house pets periodically change their favourite sleeping spots- so do Sugar Gliders. Get several pouches and nesting boxes, and tend to concentrate them at the higher end of the cage. Sugar Gliders are an arboreal (tree inhabiting) species in their natural habitat, so they naturally avoid sleeping close to the ground. They also tend to sleep together as well, but if for whatever reason one of your Sugar Gliders is in a cranky mood, they will have the option to sleep alone as well.

There is some debate about gender ratios as well. In the wild, there tends to be an alpha male, and the rest of the family are either his direct offspring or his females. If you intend on housing two males together, get them neutered. Most owners agree that you can have multiple male Sugar Gliders, as long as they are neutered. This does much to reduce the natural aggression they would otherwise have towards each other. If you keep opposite sex Sugar Gliders together and don't at least neuter the male, you will definitely have pregnant Sugar Gliders.

Unless you want joeys, please spay and neuter your Sugar Gliders. The rule of thumb is to neuter any females you don't want breeding, but in practice, an all-female colony of Sugar Gliders will not suffer from the same aggression problems as unfixed males living together will.

Chapter 6. Sugar Glider behavior and handling

Understanding the natural history and habitat of the Sugar Glider is essential to understanding your Sugar Glider as a pet. Its deep evolutionary and environmental programming informs its choices and behaviors. It is highly suggested you read on this information in Chapter 1. Once you have a solid basis for understanding where your Sugar Glider comes from (both literally and in an emotional sense), you can understand why and how your Sugar Glider does the things it does.

How sugar gliders are in the wild

Sugar Gliders are socially gregarious, tending to live in family groups in the wild. They are so named because they love licking the sugary sap of trees, although they are widely omnivorous (eating both plant and animal matter). Colonies generally reach a maximum size of 7 members, usually with a head alpha male.

They usually live in tree hollows lined with leaves, when they are not out and about foraging. They have scent glands they use to mark their territory, and usually mark their nest with urine. They give live birth to young called joeys after a brief gestation period of just over two weeks (usually between 15 to 17 days), where the joey crawls into the mothers pouch to finish further development (usually after a period of 60 to 70 days). The majority of the time, Sugar Gliders will give birth two joeys. In domestic settings, Sugar Gliders do not have a defined breeding season, but in the wild, they tend to breed during winter time.

Sugar Gliders are an animal that is typically used as an example of convergent evolution in biology classes all over the world. The superficially resemble flying squirrels (placental mammals more closely related to us than to any marsupial!) found on other continents, but in reality, natural selection chose for very similar characteristics in the only distantly related species. The niche occupied by the Sugar Glider (and flying squirrel) is that of an arboreal opportunist, leaping from tree to tree in the night time in search of insects, fruit and edible tree sap. They live in well-defined territories of up to 150 acres , and have been reported to glide between trees up to 150 feet apart (.4 ha) and males typically only live between 4 to 5 years and females live between 5 and 7 years in the wild. No worries, captive Sugar Gliders have been reported living up to 15 years (although 9 to 12 years is far more typical).

What's that sound!? About "crabbing" and other noises

So crabbing is a very distinct noise made by Sugar Gliders. It really can't be described in print very well (it is somewhere between a squeal and an electronic malfunction), so you should really look to the internet to understand exactly how it sounds. Once that is out of the way, please do *not* try and prompt this behavior from your Sugar Glider. It is a defensive noise, and you will probably hear this noise a lot when you first get your Sugar Glider. In a nutshell, it simply means your Sugar Glider is scared. Sugar Gliders are basically defenseless up close, so the sound is meant to be a bluff for predators. They may also rear up and swat or attempt to nip as part of the (attempted) intimidation routine. Don't be afraid, it can't hurt you. Once bonded to you, you will rarely hear this sound unless your Sugar Glider is startled, or intimidated by someone or something else in the room with you.

Other noises include barking, chirping and sneezing. Barking is something Sugar Gliders do like dogs- for a variety of reasons. They do it because they are lonely, bored, want your attention, excited or to bring your attention to something (or someone strange). If you want to narrow down the reason behind your Sugar Gliders barking, see what happens if you pay attention to it- if it stops, it is probably lonely. If you own a lone Sugar Glider (which you should not), it is almost certainly lonely. If you have a group barking, a veterinarian approved technique to discourage this behavior is to simply set a night light in the vicinity of their cage. They are probably barking because they are trying to locate each other, and a low level of light will help them do this. Chirping is a very soft sound they make to demonstrate they are content- this is a good sign.

You will probably hear this most after giving a nice treat to your bonded Sugar Glider. Sneezing sounds like a series of little puffs- they usually do this during grooming, and use the little puffs of air to get detritus out of their fur. If you notice them doing this sound excessively when *not* grooming (or making this noise on their genitals very frequently), you should probably consider taking them to the vet, as it may indicate a health problem with their respiratory or reproductive system.

Understanding body language

To be frank, there isn't too much to their body language. They are far too small to have expressive faces. When they are scared, they will rear up and crab. Like any other small mammal, if you notice excessive lethargy, or if it reacts poorly to being held, your Sugar Glider may be trying to tell you it is sick.

Scent marking

Males have more scent organs than do females (which are usually the case for mammals). The musky scent isn't too strong, especially when compared to other common small mammalian pets- it has been described as even being a bit fruity. That being said, males are extremely enthusiastic about scent marking- in the wild they like to establish the borders of their territory this way, so it is only natural that this behavior would carry over into captivity. Neutering a male usually makes this behavior far weaker. You will frequently see Sugar Gliders introducing themselves to each other using their scent glands. Females will rub the top of their heads on the male's scent gland. Males will likewise introduce themselves by rubbing their heads on the female's genital area and chest.

Territorial marking is usually pretty obvious because it appears somewhat like scooting. Unlike a dog scooting though, you will see the Sugar Glider scooting with his whole body- it will frankly look like dry humping. This is perfectly normal. Male Sugar Gliders will especially do this if they smell a male they do not recognize- much like dogs, they will want to claim that territory.

More you should know

Sugar Gliders can be quite energetic! This is especially true when they are in groups. Some people have even described them as being somewhat spastic. This is a good sign, it means they are happy. Naturally, they will be excited by the sight of food as well- they will clamor in your direction when they sense a meal is near. They feed in groups as well, and if your Sugar Gliders are well adjusted, there will be no fighting. You have to understand the colony tends to think of themselves as one big happy family, so there isn't much need for many feeding stations; although 2 might not be such a bad idea, as the first few might pig out and leave the rest wanting for food. It is also a good idea to have a dedicated wet food and dry food feeding station, as it helps with clean up.

Sugar Gliders are messy eaters, so unless you don't mind cleaning up the bottom of your Sugar Glider habitat often, you may want to opt for a feeding station that is contained with an overhead cover, or that they have to crawl into, just to keep the food from getting everywhere. We will discuss feeding your Sugar Glider in the upcoming section.

Chapter 7. Feeding your sugar glider

No doubt this will be the section that most excites your Sugar Glider! Sugar Gliders have an amazingly wide range of options for their diet- they are quite opportunistic in the wild and that is how they have managed to thrive. If they were excessively picky eaters, no doubt they would not be nearly as popular as pets as they are today. Indeed, it is their proclivity for eating that you as the owner should be careful of. They are prone to overeating (like all of us), and there are certain food items they should not be given for their own good. Luckily, armed with a little bit of information, they are both easy and relatively cheap to feed.

Commercially available food

There is a dizzying array of commercially available foods for your pet Sugar Glider. Often they come in brightly colored bags and with snazzy names. Just like with human food though, you need to be careful with what exactly it is you are purchasing. Your Sugar Glider has unique dietary needs and cannot be fed hamster or guinea pig pellets. They do make Sugar Glider pellets, and they are both affordable and usually pretty well balanced. You need to be sure that the food is especially formulated for Sugar Gliders, and of course, like anything else, do a little homework on the brand you are purchasing.

One danger about feeding your Sugar Glider a diet made entirely from scratch is that you will not know the exact nutritional content of the food, as you would with a lab tested pelleted food. So by being overzealous and entirely exiling pelleted foods from your Sugar Gliders diet, you may very well be causing a nutritional deficiency (or, indeed, an excess!) that can cause your animal harm. In fact, it is suggested that your Sugar Gliders diet be 75% pellets and 25% fresh foods to avoid any deleterious effects.

Brands that are generally highly recommended:
- Glider-R-Chow
- NutriMax
- VetsPride
- PocketPets

Be sure to read the labeling of the Sugar Glider pellet to appropriately follow instructions and see what supplementation is required in addition to the pellets. It varies slightly between brands.

Ensuring a balanced diet for your sugar glider

There is a wide variety of expensive diets on the internet. It's natural, some owners are a little overzealous about the nitty gritty of feeding their Sugar Gliders and only want the best of the best. Some diets even call for purchasing tree sap or gut loading insects (an idea probably borrowed from the reptile owning world)! There is no need for such excess. To be frank, most people would not keep to such elaborate diets anyway. Believe me, what you can find in the internet, a well-stocked pet store or grocery store far exceeds the needs what Sugar Gliders in the wild have access to. Understand that your Sugar Glider is a small animal and typically only consumes 30 to 60 grams of food per day per animal.

Even the most high end pelleted food (which you can usually buy by the pound/kilo) after shipping costs should keep your Sugar Glider sated for a long period of time for not very much money. Think about the last time you ate out? That one meal alone was probably more expensive than a month's supply of Sugar Glider appropriate food pellets- you do not want to cheap out with the pellets! Natural foods should be viewed primarily as an additive, and not the backbone of your Sugar Gliders diet- despite the vehement claims some owners will make on the internet.

Natural treats
With the above being said, there are a lot of natural foods you can supplement your Sugar Gliders diet with. None of the lists are absolutely exhaustive, so if there is something you would like to feed your Sugar Glider and are unsure of, feel free to reach out to your local veterinarian. A special word of caution for plant foods should be noted- make sure they are not treated with pesticides, and if you are in doubt, you have to wash such items *extremely thoroughly*, not a simple quick rinse.

Fruits
- Apples
- Apricots
- Avocado
- Bananas
- Blackberries
- Blueberries
- Cantaloupe
- Cherries (pitted)
- Coconut
- Cranberries
- Dates (pitted)
- Figs
- Grapefruit

- Grapes (seedless variety)
- Guava
- Honeydew melon
- Jackfruit
- Kiwi
- Lemon
- Lime
- Mango
- Mulberries
- Nectarine
- Oranges
- Papaya
- Passionfruit
- Peaches
- Pears
- Pineapple
- Plantain
- Plums
- Pomegranate
- Prunes (technically a plum)
- Pomelo
- Raisins (technically a grape)
- Raspberries
- Strawberries
- Tangerine
- Watermelon

Vegetables
- Alfalfa sprouts
- Artichoke
- Asparagus
- Bamboo shoots
- Beets
- Black eyed peas
- Bok Choy
- Broccoli
- Brussels sprouts
- Cabbage
- Carrots
- Cauliflower
- Celery
- Chicory Greens
- Collard Greens
- Jicama

- Kale
- Lettuce
- Mustard Greens
- Okra
- Peas
- Potato
- Pumpkin
- Radish
- Rutabagas
- Snow peas
- Spinach
- Summer Squash
- Swiss chard
- Turnip
- Watercress
- Yams (cooked)
- Zucchini

Meat
This is an element of the diet that should be fed sparingly at best. Just be sure it is lean and cooked thoroughly. Although Sugar Gliders have been known to eat small reptiles and mammals in the wild, our meat sources are different from their wild cousin's sources. On that note, keep your small pet reptiles away from your Sugar Gliders for this reason!

- Fish
- Poultry
- Pork
- Red meat

Miscellaneous
- Artificial nectar mix (Leadbeater's mixture, in particular)
- Corn
- Eggs (boiled or otherwise cooked)
- Honey
- Mushrooms
- Nuts (very occasionally, as they are high in calories)
- Pure fruit juices (no added sugars)
- White rice (cooked)

Insects
As discussed earlier, since insects will not be forming the backbone of your Sugar Gliders diet, there is no need to "gut load" your insects prior to feeding them to your Sugar Glider. The insects you do decide to feed to

your Sugar Glider should come from the pet store - you do not know the provenance of the wild insects running loose in your house or yard (and what nasty diseases or chemicals they may have come into contact with). Whether or not you feed your Sugar Gliders live insects or dead ones is up to you.

Insects
- Butterworm
- Crickets
- Dubia roach
- Fly pupae
- Hissing cockroach
- Mealworms

NOTE: Special care should be taken to avoid feeding your Sugar Glider crickets raised on corn mash.

Vitamins and supplements

When feeding pelleted foods, please read the instructions for your particular brand. Some may not be nutritionally complete without the addition of that particular brand supplements (sometimes they will call the additional supplement a "gravy"). You may also consider adding a multivitamin supplement to the Sugar Gliders diet as well, but be sure it is Sugar Glider appropriate. Such supplements can usually be added to fruits, veggies, pellets and living insects.

Rather than sprinkle your supplement on the insects like you would a piece of fruit or vegetable, some people will actually put the ultrafine power in a container with the live insects and let them roam around in it so there is adheres to their exoskeleton. Clearly dead insects, you can just sprinkle the powder on.

Excessive phosphorus has been linked to metabolic bone disease in Sugar Gliders, which can ultimately be fatal to your Sugar Glider. All living things need phosphorus in their diets, so please don't overdo it and exclude it entirely from your Sugar Glider's diet- this will *certainly* kill your pet. It is not so much an overdose of phosphorus that is dangerous, rather, it has to do with the ratio of phosphorus to calcium in the Sugar Gliders diet.

This is why it is crucial to buy a multivitamin or supplement made with Sugar Gliders in mind, as the necessary ratio of phosphorous to calcium varies between different species. We will get into the nitty gritty of this in the malady section of this book. They do make and sell specific supplements that take into account the proper amount of phosphorus your Sugar Glider should consume.

Dangerous foods

Please remember that although the Sugar Glider is an opportunistic omnivorous mammal, much like us, it is *not* a human being! There are certainly foods that we consume that will either harm or kill your Sugar Glider, just like with other pets.

Foods that are poisonous to Sugar Gliders
- Alcohol
- Anything with caffeine
- Chocolate
- Chives
- Fruit pits
- House plants
- Garlic
- Leeks
- Onions

All the above foods are outright poisonous. Caffeine is actually a neurostimulant that most animals cannot properly metabolize, including Sugar Gliders, so coffee and tea are prohibited. Fruit pits have been known to contain trace amounts of cyanide, which although are harmless to animals with large body volumes (you would have to eat thousands to feel any ill effects), they can be deadly to small animals, such as Sugar Gliders. Most animals cannot metabolize chives, garlic, leeks or onion like human beings can- they all belong to the plant genus *Allium* which contain a class of chemicals called organosulfoxides.

This class of compounds, or their metabolites (what the body processes the chemicals into) can cause severe damage to the blood cells of most pets, including your Sugar Gliders. Blood is what carries oxygen to your tissue, so it is a bit of a big deal if blood cells get damaged en masse. Humans just happen to have the appropriate enzymes to deal with the organosulfoxides this genus of plants contains, your Sugar Glider does not. Houseplants should never be fed to any pet- the majority are poisonous to people, let alone animals. Alcohol, hopefully, should speak for itself as to why it is on this list.

Foods to be avoided or fed in moderation
You will see an overlap with this section and some of the foods in the acceptable category- this is not a mistake. Sugar Glider diets should adhere

to some common sense guidelines, especially about what foods they can definitely eat in excess. A single donut will not harm a person, but eating a dozen a day over an extended period of time will- the same applies to your Sugar Glider. Obesity in Sugar Gliders has more or less the same effects on them as it does in human beings- liver, heart and joint problems. The only difference is, we get a say in our diets, and your Sugar Glider does not.

Since Sugar Gliders have shorter lifespans as well, they will succumb to the ill effects of obesity more rapidly as well. Even healthy foods should be portioned out appropriately- a single grape seems small to us, but compared to a Sugar Glider, it is like a watermelon!

- Processed sugars- These are to be avoided entirely, just like in us. In extreme moderation, a one off is not lethal, just as in human beings. It is a great way to make Sugar Gliders picky eaters and to make them obese in a hurry, though.

- Carbohydrates- For example, bread or potatoes, low in nutrition, high in calories, probably the second worst non-lethal food you can give to Sugar Gliders after outright processed Sugars.

- Dairy products- Cheese and ice cream- Sugar Gliders do not have the right enzyme to properly digest these products, and are thus considered lactose intolerant. Oddly, however, a small amount of yogurt is not associated with ill effects for Sugar Gliders.

- All fruits- Very high in sugars, but most complex sugars, so not as calorie dense as processed sugars. This is the treat you can most often give your Sugar Glider. Also, highly textured fruit may have pesticide residue that is extremely difficult to wash out.

- Nuts- They are very healthy, but extremely calorie dense, a tremendous source of fats. They should only be given as special treats occasionally.

- All protein sources- Insect or otherwise- think of what will happen to you if you eat dozens of hamburgers a week. They perhaps don't have to be treated like a rare treat, but give them protein as often as an average person would eat bacon. Everyone knows bacon everyday isn't good for you, but every once in a while isn't a showstopper either.

- Syrups- Canned fruit syrup, maple syrup or even honey! They are all just gooey versions of regular sugar. They may have more vitamins and nutrients in them than regular table sugar, but the amount of calories packed in them reserves this class of food into strictly the treat category.

It's never a bad thing to treat your pets. However, as we all know, there is too much of a good thing. Follow human guidelines for treating your Sugar Gliders- special occasions (during human holidays, moving into a larger cage, after the successful birth of joeys, etc.), after an illness, common sense moderation. Your Sugar Glider is entirely at your mercy for its diet, you can kill with kindness just as easily as with ignorance.

Chapter 8. Play and Exercise

This is probably the section of the book you as the owner are most looking forward to. Rejoice! Sugar Gliders love to play and are very active animals. They will also need attention from you as the owner, play mates and toys to interact with for enrichment purposes to reach their maximum potential as Sugar Gliders. Remember, they cover a lot of ground out in the wild, so chances are they will not have the same amount of space in your home or in their enclosure with which to burn off all that excess energy. Play is an excellent way to exercise your Sugar Glider and to ensure its health.

Playing with your Sugar Glider

Please remember your Sugar Glider is much smaller than you are and has a pretty fragile bone structure. For this reason, strictly supervise, or even entirely prevent, play with small children. Small children are still learning the basics about the world, and the concept that a small animal cannot take rough housing the same way another pet could (like a larger dog) probably has not entered their mind. They may accidentally break a Sugar Gliders bones or even kill it through blunt force trauma. It would be heart breaking for you, the Sugar Glider's colony (they are social, remember) and the child to experience this.

More space is better for play with your Sugar Glider. Some owners have gone as far as to purchase camping tents to let their sugar glider loose into (indoors) to let them jump over a larger space. There is nothing wrong with this, but I suspect most owners would not go this far in acquiring items for their Sugar Glider. A room with minimal obstructions and soft landing spaces is probably ideal to let them run around (and of course, glide) in. Most people's living rooms suffice, in so far as you closely supervise them.

There is a small chance that Sugar Gliders may confuse some wooden furniture for trees, so make sure they have a chance to scope out such furniture first before you let them glide towards it. If the furniture is slick, they may glide, slip to the ground and injure themselves. They are small curious creatures and will like to explore. They may find an electrical outlet, or other small dangerous places to stick their hands into, so please watch your Sugar Glider. Some basic baby proofing can go a long way in ensuring your Sugar Glider has a safe space to explore in your home.

In terms of playing environment, there are a few things to consider. Please do not let your Sugar Glider play in the bathroom or kitchen- there are many hazards in both areas. You would be surprised the amount of Sugar Gliders that get killed by drowning in unattended sinks or toilet bowls. Not a pleasant sight to behold. There are also things that may smell or taste interesting to Sugar Gliders in those rooms that are lethal to consume (food items that are prohibited, soaps, pest baits, etc.).

You should also clean up whatever room you're playing in with your Sugar Glider. Easily nibbled plastics should be removed (Ziploc bags, grocery store bags, potato chip bags, etc.), as they may ingest some of it, and if it ends up stuck in your Sugar Glider's digestive system, you will definitely end up with an expensive veterinarian bill, or, worst case scenario, a dead Sugar Glider.

Sharp objects obviously should be removed, and mugs filled with liquid, surprisingly enough. I have witnessed it myself, a Sugar Glider will glide to a mug filled with, say, coffee, somehow manage *not* to knock it over and end up face first in the drink. Usually this just results in a mess for all parties involved, but it is a drowning risk, and even if they just inhale some in a panic, it could harm their respiratory system. Never mind if they ingest something inappropriate for them (like coffee).

You should also remove potentially predatory pets! Clearly you know your other pets better than anyone else, but it is probably best to remove cats and dogs from your Sugar Gliders vicinity, at least at first. Young animals (kittens and puppies especially) have the strongest predatory/play drives, and cannot be trusted with your Sugar Glider. Your Sugar Glider looks exactly like what most animals would hunt in the wild - small, furry and rapidly moving. Even if your animal means no harm, chances are it is way bigger and stronger than your Sugar Glider.

A cat's nails may be an annoyance to you, but are like steak knives to a Sugar Glider. Getting hit with a dog paw is probably somewhat like getting hit with a sledge hammer to the Sugar Glider. Birds beaks hurt when they bite you as a person, imagine what happens to a Sugar Glider's delicate bones, yikes!

As for gliding, probably the best place to try your f initial forays into it are in the cage's vicinity. The Sugar Glider is already familiar with the properties of your cage, and should be familiar with the properties of your clothing if you have bonded with it. Try putting your Sugar Glider on or on top of the cage and walking a few paces away to try and prompt it you glide to you. You may also do vice versa. After this, you can try on another surface (from you to a couch, for example). They aren't called Sugar Gliders for nothing.

Common Household Hazards (List)
- Toilets
- Sinks
- Household cleaners
- Air fresheners
- Candles
- Scented disinfectant wipes
- Insect baits and traps
- Poisoned insects
- Gasoline (on your hand, especially)
- Tap water (sometimes utilities will spike chlorine or fluoride to clean pipes, although harmless to people, it is lethal to Sugar Gliders)
- Pots & pans
- Electrical outlets

Toys

Toys should be bought for your Sugar Glider to interact with. We have already spoken about the important of an exercise wheel earlier in the book (under the accessories section) - please go back and read that section to know exactly what to get in terms of an exercise wheel. It is so important in fact, it cannot in good consciousness be classed as merely a toy- it is an essential piece of equipment for proper Sugar Glider husbandry. Buying the wrong exercise wheel could very easily kill your Sugar Glider. Everything else after the exercise wheel is an extra to keep your Sugar Glider properly enriched.

Easy toy options can be found in the bird and small mammal section of your local pet store. It is suggested you take the bell off all toys you do happen to buy, because the Sugar Gliders will be playing with their toys primarily at night - probably when you want to sleep the most. You can also buy toys with the aim of hiding treats in them to challenge your Sugar Gliders to forage a bit, as they would in the wild naturally, anyway.

If you are a little more adventurous, you can also buy a little storage container, cut holes into (make sure to tape around the holes to keep sharp edges to a minimum) and put plush toys and balls in it. The Sugar Gliders will treat it as a child treats a ball pit. Just be aware you are going to have to clean this option out periodically. If you do buy any toys utilizing wood, steer clear of cedar and pine, as these are toxic to your Sugar Gliders as earlier discussed.

Popular Toy Options
- Swings
- Hide-a-treat boxes
- Hide-a-treat globes
- Plush balls
- Plush toys
- "Kabob" toys (basically rope strung through food or other items)
- Ladders
- Nesting fleece strips

Weight loss

If your Sugar Glider should be on the pudgy side - see if you have enough toys in its habitat. Maybe your Sugar Glider has special needs (if it is older, maybe focus on buying ramps more than swings, for example). All Sugar Gliders have their own personalities, so you will need to do a gut check to see what toys and accessories you feel are appropriate for your Sugar Gliders activity level.

If you consider your Sugar Glider obese, it is best you take it in to the veterinarian to come up with a game plan on how to correct your Sugar Glider's weight problem.

Habitat features

Habitat Enriching Features

There are many, many add-ons you can attach to your cage to make it a more stimulating habitat for your Sugar Gliders. The wild forests of Australasia (where they are native to) are varied in nature, so should their captive environments.

These are structural features you should seriously consider adding to your cage to make it a more interesting place to live:
- Meshed platforms to walk on
- Climbing ledges
- Meshed nesting boxes
- Connecting tunnels (to connect to other cages!)
- Meshed exercise ramps
- Meshed arches (basically a connecting tunnel that goes on the top of cages)
- Dry moss (for nesting materials)

Plant Branches

Plant branches are a wonderful addition to a habitat, although you need to be very careful about what kind of plant matter you allow your Sugar Gliders to come in to contact with. It is not suggested that you keep live plants (even if they were compatible with your Sugar Gliders health) simply for logistical reasons. They may eat the dirt, knock it over, uproot it or simply gnaw the plant to death anyways. Best to bring in plant parts!

Acceptable branch species

Again, this list is not exhaustive. If you should have any doubts about the species you intend to use, please err on the side of caution and discuss it with a reputable Sugar Glider dealer, rescue agency or a veterinarian. Please be absolutely sure that the branches you intend to use have not been treated against parasites, with fertilizers or other potentially harmful chemicals before you harvest them. The leaves are fine to leave on the branches and will make for ideal nesting material for your Sugar Glider to harvest.

- Apple trees
- Aspen trees
- Citrus species (orange trees, lime trees, lemon trees, etc.)
- Cottonwood trees
- Eucalyptus trees
- Hibiscus bush
- Willow trees

Unacceptable branch species

To reiterate, please, err on the side of caution. This is a sort of greatest hits list of plants you should *not harvest* branches from for your Sugar Glider habitat. If you have any doubts, reach out to the wider Sugar Glider community or your veterinarian for clarification. I am positive there are thousands of other species of plants that would be harmful to your Sugar Glider. In general, avoid any sappy plants (whether they be coniferous or deciduous).

- Almond trees
- Apricot trees
- Black walnut trees
- Cherry trees
- Peach trees
- Any sort of pine tree

Chapter 9. Hygiene

More good news! Sugar Gliders are very conscientious about their hygiene. This is critical for their social functions as well, very much like human beings. The easiest thing for you to do as an owner to promote proper hygiene with your Sugar Glider, is to simply keep its surroundings clean. Much like it is very difficult for a human being to stay clean if their home is dirty, it is the same thing with Sugar Gliders. For most (but not all other things), Sugar Gliders will basically take care of themselves in this field of care.

Sugar glider grooming

Sugar Gliders will instinctively groom themselves. After eating, playing and sleeping it is the most common activity to see them engaging in. The grooming consists of them licking their own fur while making the sneezing noise discussed earlier in the book. Since Sugar Gliders are socially gregarious creatures, they will often groom other members of their colony as well. It helps them bond with the other Sugar Gliders they are housed with.

Bathing (if necessary)

Sugar Gliders are extremely clean animals, and it is possible to have Sugar Gliders without ever bathing themselves. If for whatever reason you do smell a strong musk of sorts, it is probably more related to their diet than any sort of grooming issue, so you should consult your veterinarian as to the correct course of action regarding their food intake. After this has been considered and you insist on bathing your Sugar Gliders, there are two simple techniques to bathe them.

The first, and easiest and safest way to bathe a Sugar Glider is to simply pat them down with a baby wipe. If it is gentle enough for a baby, it is usually gentle enough for a Sugar Glider. If you insist on a more thorough bathing technique, then you can wash them down with a *small* amount of warm water and baby shampoo in a bathing bowl. The water must be *very* shallow as Sugar Gliders entirely lack any sort of swimming instinct whatsoever, and can drown extremely easily. You should not take your eyes off them for even a moment when they are near a body of liquid larger than they are.

Trimming nails

Sugar Gliders need extremely sharp, fast growing nails to survive in the wild. There is no point to Sugar Gliders gliding long distances between trees if they cannot grasp the bark and fall to their deaths. Sharp claws are an essential tool for them to land safely after takeoff. In a domestic setting though, overly sharp or long nails can be uncomfortable for both the Sugar Glider and whomever they come into contact with!

You should never clip your Sugar Gliders toe nails, unless a veterinarian compels you too. Their nails are so small, you are almost certain to hit the quick of the nail without extreme care. Also, Sugar Gliders have an instinctual psychological compulsion to make sure they have a firm grip on their surroundings. Severely clipped nails will prevent them from having a solid grasp on anything around them (their cage, toys, pouches, etc.) and cause them tremendous anxiety. There is a better way to deal with their nails.

Filing is the solution. Gently file the nails down until it feels comfortable on your skin, and you can tell your Sugar Glider will still have a good grip on things in its environment. You can do this manually, with a regular old nail file and file down each nail one at a time. Usually, to use this method, it takes two people. One person holds the Sugar Glider, and holds one of the paws splayed out, the other person gently files the nails (as a whole, not individually) with a nail file in a gentle sweeping motion. It should only take a few swipes to make the Sugar Glider's nails manageable on each paw. If you happen to over file, your Sugar Glider will feel anxiety as it maneuvers its environment.

If for whatever reason you happen to hit their quick, you should have a styptic powder handy (like QuikStop) to stop the bleeding. No worries, the nails grow back extremely quickly, which is why you need to file their nails approximately once a week or so.

An easier (some would even say, automatic) way to file your Sugar Gliders nails though is to put "trim tracks" into their exercise wheel. A trim track is an abrasive insert (a Sugar Glider specialized kind of sandpaper, if you will) that is designed to wear down the Sugar Gliders nails as they run on the exercise wheel. Please do not cheap out and try to use industrial sandpaper in your exercise wheel- you will injure your Sugar Glider and prevent it from using it's much needed exercise wheel.

Chapter 10: Health

The overall health of your Sugar Glider is of paramount importance to your ownership and happiness with the Sugar Glider. The overwhelming majority of cases involving sick Sugar Gliders visiting the vet are usually tied to poor diet. Malnutrition and obesity (or for some particularly unlucky Sugar Gliders, both simultaneously) are far and away the biggest killers of Sugar Gliders in captivity today. Please be sure to pay extra special attention to the diet section earlier in this book - this will save you and your Sugar Glider a tremendous amount of suffering and time. Most other emergency trips to the veterinarian's office involve injuries sustained from Sugar Glider activities.

This is simply a matter of making sure the habitat is set up properly and that they do not come into contact with any hazardous obstacles or substances. The most common hazards encountered by Sugar Gliders was also discussed at length earlier in this book, so please review them. This section is primarily to help you get an idea of how your Sugar Glider is built, what is normal for them physically and an explanation of particularly common afflictions that may be making them ill (and how to recognize them).

Basic anatomy

A History Lesson first
Sugar Gliders are marsupials, so they have some pretty unique physiological quirks. On the surface, they seem quite like a rodent (like squirrels, but particularly like flying squirrels). Nothing could be further from the truth. At a taxonomic and genetic level, you are more closely related to a flying squirrel than a Sugar Glider. Mammals can be broadly classified into three classes (scientifically, actually an "infraclass") - marsupials, placental mammals and monotremes. To keep it brief and informative, marsupials have external pouches their young develop to completion in (they have a comparatively very brief internal gestation period, and are born in a fetal stage and crawl to the pouch). Think kangaroos, opossums, koalas and yes, our friend, the Sugar Glider. The vast majority of marsupial species are found in Australia, although there are a few in the Americas as well (like the Virginia Opossum).

Monotremes are a handful of mammalian species (oddly, all found only in Australia) that lay eggs. Placental mammals are the types of mammals you are most familiar with, their young develop attached to a placenta within their mothers and are born fully formed (if small). This includes species such as cats, dogs, elephants, dolphins, bats and human beings. The truth of the matter is the last common ancestor any placental mammal shared with any marsupial was during the early Cretaceous Period (sometime between 100 and 145 million years ago, when dinosaurs were very much still alive).

All placental mammals had a common ancestor more recently, about 66 million years ago. This means you are more closely related to all other placental mammals (including the flying squirrel) than your Sugar Glider is related to any placental mammal at all. You are indeed, very distant cousins.

Anatomical features most marsupials have
- Front pouch where nipples and young are housed for development
- The presence of epipubic bones - bones that project forward from the pelvic bones (they are to support the weight of the pouch and young). Uniquely among marsupials, these are either greatly diminished or entirely lacking in Sugar Gliders, which is thought to be an evolutionary feature to reduce weight and aid with gliding.
- Lack a corpus callosum linking the two (right and left) hemispheres of the brain together
- Typically have many more teeth than placental mammals

Basic Anatomical features of your Sugar Glider

What makes it glide?
Let's start with the most obvious feature of your Sugar Glider- the part that makes it glide. The flaps, wings, whatever you call them actually have a scientific name- the patagium. It is pronounced as "pah-tay-jee-um". It is simply a zoological term to describe a membrane or fold of skin between the forelimbs and hind limbs on each side of the animal that assists with flight or gliding.

When the Sugar Glider extends its limbs apart after a jump, the membrane is designed to increase the surface area of your Sugar Glider that can capture and direct air to help it glide. It is also a large part of why Sugar Gliders cannot even attempt to swim- imagine if you had large membranes between your wrists and ankles - you would drown in a hurry as well. The patagium is just a soft tissue membrane - there are no ligaments or bones in it like a batwing.

Look at those eyes!
Sugar Gliders are nocturnal, so they have very large brown eyes, especially when compared to their body size. Their eyes will open at 12 to 13 weeks of age. It is unknown whether Sugar Gliders have color vision, although most scientific inquiries into whether or not nocturnal animals possess color vision finds they very often do not (who can see colors at night anyway?). Very typically, nocturnal animals have far more rods (receptors used for contrast in dark environments) than cones (the receptors within the eyes used to distinguish colors apart) - anatomical dissections of marsupial gliders eyes have revealed this is true for them as well.

Your Sugar Glider also has one more eye feature that you should be aware of- the tapetum lucidum. It is a reflective layer of pigment inside your Sugar Gliders eye that allows it to more efficiently collect light in the dark. Why should you pay special mind to this feature you ask? If you should ever lose your Sugar Glider, you can try to "spotlight" it by shining your flashlight at it. If you see two glowing eyes staring back at you from the dark in your house or yard, and you recently lost your Sugar Glider, chances are pretty solid you just found your pet again. Of course, exercise common sense and don't wander into the woods after every pair of glowing eyes you see in the dark (you may stumble upon an angry raccoon that way!). Your Sugar Glider's "eye shine" will be reddish orange in color.

What large ears!
Yes, your Sugar Glider will have two large ears. Although they are endearing in purpose, they serve an evolutionarily important role for your Sugar Glider. When operating in low light environments, hearing can be just as important as sight - especially when on the hunt for insects! If you think you can hear bugs crawling, I can guarantee that your Sugar Glider hears it way better. They do have the ability to move their ears independently of each other, so they can listen to a much larger effective area than animals that cannot do this (like us!). In addition to being a hunting aid, it is also a great defense from predators, especially birds of prey that might come thundering down from the canopy.

What soft fur!
Like most other small mammals, the Sugar Glider has a body covered in soft fur. Its topside is usually a grey color, with notable black stripes running from head to tail. In recent years, new color morphs have been bred into the captive Sugar Glider population, which will be described in the list below. Wild Sugar Gliders though are always grey- this helps it

camouflage against the bark of the trees in its natural habitat. The bottom of your Sugar Glider will be a light cream color.

Common Color Morphs amongst captive Sugar Gliders
- Albino- All white with red eyes

- Black beauty- Looks very much like a classic Sugar Glider, just the darker portions are extremely dark.

- Caramels- They have a similar appearance to standard Sugar Gliders, the grey color is light enough to have a beige like appearance. These usually belong to the subspecies of *Petaurus breviceps flavidus* and originally hail from the southern portion of the island of New Guinea.

- Classic- The vast majority of the Sugar Gliders you will encounter will have this color morph. Typical grey appearance, with the black stripe, dark eyes and cream colored bottom.

- Cremeino- Although similar in appearance at first glance to the albino morph, cremeinos have slightly more pigmentation in their fur (hence cream colored, versus all white) and have red eyes.

- Leucistic- All white fur, very light colored ears and normal dark eyes.

- Mosaic- Multicolored. Any unusual colored patch of fur can label a Sugar Glider as piebald (from an all-black Sugar Glider with a light patch of fur to vice versa)

- Platinum- All fur color features have been significantly "toned down" in this morph. The fur appears to have a silver appearance and stripes are faded. Like a lighter colored caramel morph.

- Reds & Strawberries- Eyes appear reddish (think of a toned down albino) with a reddish hued fur.

- Ruby Leucistic/ Ruby Platinum- Leucistic fur with albino red eyes.

- White face blonde- Basically, a normal morph Sugar Glider, although lacking the dark strip feature in the facial region

- Melanistic- All black/dark brown fur.

- White tip- Normal Sugar Glider morph, but with a white capped tail.

The hands (or paws)
Sugar Gliders have very agile hands - they superficially resemble primate hands. This is because both monkeys and Sugar Gliders inhabit a pretty similar niche - they live amongst tree canopies and need to navigate on or through thin branches consistently. The front and back feet/paws/hands however are not absolutely identical however. A unique feature of their hands is the typically marsupial feature of having the second and third toes (counting from the "thumb") of the back hand/foot/paw joined together. This superficially makes it look like one large toe with a split nail. It is a unique adaptation, the syndactylous toes (which is the proper scientific term for the feature) are usually used for grooming purposes in marsupials.

Watch your Sugar Glider closely - he will use his fused second and third toe somewhat how we would use a comb. Your Sugar Glider will lick it and run it through its fur. Each hand of the Sugar Glider also has a toe that is similar in function to a human thumb - it is opposable, which works wonders for their (and our) grip. All the toes have sharp claws.

A cute nose
Your Sugar Glider, regardless of its morph, will have a pink nose. They do have a fantastic sense of smell, and have a seemingly bottomless curiosity. When encountering something new, they will sniff it first, and then try to eat it to test its edibility. This is why you have to be careful what your Sugar Glider is exposed to in your home.

The mouth
Just like us, they have a tongue and teeth in their mouth. This is about where the similarity ends. In the dental world, Sugar Gliders are classified as diprotodonts, meaning they have prominent mandibular central incisors (i.e. In plain English, the two middle teeth in the lower jaw are prominently longer than the other teeth). This is not a feature unique to Sugar Gliders (although the Sugar Glider has developed its own use for this feature), rather, it is a defining feature of the predominant class of marsupials than inhabit the Australasia region.

Species as diverse as kangaroos, koalas, wombats and even the now extinct Thylacine (Tasmanian Tiger) belong to this class. These two teeth are used by Sugar Gliders in the wild as a sort of scooper to help them scrape fruit and sap easily. Unlike rodents, these teeth do not continuously grow during their lifespan, so they should not be in any way trimmed down. Their teeth are as permanent as ours! The tongue has no special feature, other than it is rather long, probably ideal for licking up vast quantities of sap.

The tail
An extremely prominent feature making up about half of the Sugar Glider's body length, the tail is extremely important for Sugar Glider navigation in the wild. While it may just appear as a cute appendage to us, it plays a central role in the Sugar Glider's movements. Its primary function is to aid in the Sugar Glider's balance while moving through the tree tops and to help it better navigate through the air (think of a primitive rudder) when gliding. The tail is semi-prehensile, meaning it has limited grasping abilities.

For example, you may see the Sugar Glider holding on to a food item with it, or grasping onto a tree branch or cage feature to angle itself better to get at food. It is not very strong though - a full prehensile tail, like that found on monkeys, would allow it to support its entire body weight while hanging from it. Sugar Gliders cannot do this, and also for this reason, you should never treat your Sugar Gliders tail like a handle to carry it around. You will cause it great pain and discomfort and you will probably very severely injure your Sugar Glider.

Sexing your sugar glider
You would think it would be obvious sexing your Sugar Glider- I mean, just look at its bottom and see - boy or girl? You know what you are looking for. Well - it should be emphasized, Sugar Gliders are unique. Marsupials have a different genitalia set up than placental mammals, and sexing Sugar Gliders is not as easy as simply looking for a penis or vagina, like you would for most of your other furry pets.

Male Sugar Gliders : Non Sexual Features
First we will discuss the unique non-genitalia features of your male Sugar Glider. Male Sugar Gliders have three scent glands which leave unique marks depending on their placement on the Sugar Gliders body. The first scent gland is located on the top of the head, when your Sugar Glider is fully grown, this spot will bald. The second scent gland is located on the chest area, which will cause the fur in that area to take a somewhat orange hue. The third area is in the vicinity of the anus. Males are usually 24-30 (9 to 12 inches) cm in length from nose to tip of tail when fully grown.

Male Sugar Gliders : Sexual Features
The penis and testicles will not be obvious to you, the layperson. Assuming your Sugar Glider is fully mature, if you flip him over, you will notice one large sack. It just looks like a lump covered in fur. The testicles are in here. The penis is not readily visible. It is hidden within the cloaca (the slit below the testicles, at the base of the tail) of the Sugar Glider. Notice

something about this ordering. You will only see it when it is aroused and pops out of the cloaca. The penis is *below* the testicles, quite unlike the genitals of human beings. This is the typical ordering for most Australasian marsupials however.

There is one more unique feature you should know about your Sugar Gliders penis. It is bifurcated. That means it has two heads, some could say it resembles a serpents tongue. The bifurcation starts near the "stem" of the penis if you will, so a bit of the penis looks like two fused penises as the base, and splits up the closer you get to the head. Of course it is pink in color. This is important to know as there are anecdotal cases floating about on the internet where owners have panicked thinking their Sugar Glider had a worm or parasite problem and have attempted to remove the penis.

Don't do this. This is the natural appearance of your male Sugar Gliders penis, and it lines up perfectly with your female Sugar Gliders anatomy (yes, there is a double vagina, more on that in the female section). Also, unlike human beings, urethra (the tube where urine comes out of) of the male Sugar Glider ends near the base of where the penis bifurcates, not at the heads. Male marsupials do not have nipples. Male Sugar Gliders typically reach sexual maturity a little over a year after leaving their mother's pouch, and thus reach full adulthood more slowly than their female counterparts.

Female Sugar Gliders : Nonsexual features
Sugar Gliders are a sexually dimorphic species, so female Sugar Gliders are smaller in appearance than male Sugar Gliders. Apart from this, they cannot be readily sexed without looking at the genital areas, although some would say the females have a softer appearance.

Female Sugar Gliders : Sexual Features
Where the testicles would be on a male Sugar Glider, the female will have its pouch. The formal name of the pouch is the marsupium, and it contains four teats (nipples), from which young one or two joeys will select from and suckle upon for milk. The vagina of the Sugar Glider, just like the penis of the male Sugar Glider, is a little more complicated than its human counterpart. The vagina is also bifurcated (hence the males unique penis structure). There are two vaginal tracts that unite into a single canal within the Sugar Glider (clearly, out of our view). Of special note, the bifurcated vaginal tubes twist around the urethral tube in the female. This is important for your veterinarian to know when the time to spay your Sugar Glider comes- there have been reports of urethral damage during the hysterectomy procedure. For this reason (amongst many others), you should seek out the

professional guidance of an exotic animal veterinarian - a regular veterinarian may not be aware of this fact.

Vaccinations, spaying & neutering and breeding your Sugar Gliders

As stated earlier in the book, an ounce of prevention is worth a ton of cure. Vaccines are usually top of the list when it comes to preventative care for your pets- this is not the case with Sugar Gliders (we will cover this in detail below). Aside from nutritional concerns, which have been exhaustively covered in prior chapters, your biggest worry should be spaying and neutering your Sugar Gliders. It's understood many people love their Sugar Gliders, and would love nothing more than to see tons of joeys (in case you have not caught on at this point in the book, that is the term for marsupial babies) running around the enclosure. They are quite a sight to see. However, there are already too many unwanted, mistreated and abandoned Sugar Gliders in the world.

Do serious self-examination if you really want to bring new animals in to this world- you are *entirely* responsible for the lives of the animals you already own as well as the new animals. Unless you are ready for the logistics and responsibilities of breeding your animals, and have exhaustively researched every aspect of joey husbandry, please do not permit your Sugar Gliders to breed. Aside from ethical concerns, there may also be legal restrictions on the breeding of Sugar Gliders where you live. That being said, we will discuss a little about the procedures to "fix" your Sugar Glider.

Vaccinations

Sugar Gliders do not need vaccines! Vaccines are a wonderful, marvelous piece of biological technology and highly recommended by both animal veterinarians and human doctors alike for a reason. Why doesn't your Sugar Glider need a vaccine then? Frankly, because of its fundamentally exotic nature.

Sugar Gliders are relatively new to contact with human beings. Even the earliest relations between Sugar Gliders and the Indigenous Australians had more of a predator-prey dynamic than a modern pet-owner dynamic to it. Sugar Gliders have never (until *very* recently, biologically speaking) been bred in confined spaces in large numbers. In fact, there are no truly domesticated marsupial species to this day- even the Sugar Glider itself is more of a docile wild animal than a truly domesticated animal with an inherent fondness for human beings, like say, a dog. Why else would you need to devote time and energy to bonding and stopping their crabbing behavior? Puppies are all over you from the very beginning, because that is how dogs have been selectively bred for thousands of years and countless generations. Sugar Gliders are a practically brand new species when it comes to time spent in captivity. Sugar Gliders have had many tens of thousands of years living at relatively low population densities in their natural habitat - hardly the environment for a contagious epidemic to evolve.

More importantly, it is because they are marsupials. They are at best, extremely distantly related to the wide variety of common household and domesticated farm animals we associate with a variety of illnesses. It is this evolutionary isolation that is key to their unique immune system. You see, it is not that Sugar Gliders (or other marsupials for that matter) have particularly strong immune systems, it is just that they are *different from* our branch of mammals. Bacteria and viruses are just like any other set of organisms- they have evolved to work within certain environments and parameters.

When they are introduced to a situation that is outside of their bounds, usually they (the bacteria and viruses) die. The fact of the matter is that Australasian marsupials and the vast majority of placental mammals (there are bats, seals and whales in Australasia, you have to remember) have been isolated for a very long time, so their body chemistry and metabolism is, from the microorganisms perspective, pretty dissimilar.

Ok then, you ask - "If pathogenic (which means illness causing) organisms just die when they attempt to jump species, why do our pets need so many vaccines to prevent them from spreading disease to people?". The key word is *usually*. Evolution is all about statistics - the more often one species of microorganism is introduced to an animal, the better the chance that there will be a mutant *who can* take root in the new host (the animal in question). Humans have been hunting with dogs for tens of thousands of years, herding sheep and cattle for many thousands of years, etcetera. It is a function of time- the more time two populations of animals spend with each other, the more likely the microorganism they have will be able to crossover. Human beings, and indeed, all placental mammals and Sugar Gliders just have not been around each other in close contact for that long.

A good counter example would be chickens and human beings able to exchange the flu virus. There is no way a human being is more closely related to a chicken than to a Sugar Glider. That is correct- chickens are way less closely related to human beings than Sugar Gliders, so what gives with the ability to share the flu virus? The key ingredient is time. Chickens were domesticated from Indian Jungle fowl thousands and thousands of years ago, and countless billions of human beings and countless billions of chickens have been interacting in billions of ways in close confines in not always very sanitary conditions- it was inevitable from a statistical point of view.

I can guarantee you there have not been billions of Sugar Gliders in the entire natural history of the species, and certainly billions of people have not interacted with them. Indeed, there probably have not been billions of interactions between Sugar Gliders and *any* placental mammals whatsoever- hence the lack of diseases that can be easily communicable between us (or other pets) and our Sugar Gliders. No diseases that can be shared means no vaccines can be developed for Sugar Gliders, means no vaccines will need to be administered to our furry friends. Maybe in the distant future this will change - but for now, you as the owner are in the clear.

Spaying and neutering
Now on to the more pressing concern about unwanted reproduction. If you have a fertile male and a fertile female in close confines to each other, there is a 100% guarantee you *will* have joeys. Do not for a second think this is something you can put off. These Sugar Gliders (like you and I) are the direct result of billions of ancestors getting it on - the instinct to have sex is just as deeply ingrained in them as it is in any one of us. Sugar Gliders have about as much impulse control as you can expect from any animal - zero. If you have a colony of females and a fertile male in their presence - you will have *multiple* new joeys to contend with.

Neutering is the easier procedure to perform - aside from the unique appearance from Sugar Gliders' testicles, the procedure is relatively straightforward and quite similar to those performed on placental mammals such as cats, dogs and guinea pigs. For female Sugar Gliders, spaying is slightly more complicated. As mentioned earlier in the section on sexual features of female Sugar Gliders - the vagina of Sugar Gliders is bifurcated and within the body of the Sugar Glider, the vagina twists around the urethral tube (this is the tube that carries urine away from the bladder- *very important!*).

Although all licensed veterinarians are educated responsible professionals, one that may not be familiar with this anatomical quirk may very well damage the urethra during the hysterectomy procedure. For this reason, it is strongly suggested than when the time for spaying your Sugar Glider comes- you take it to an exotic animal specialist. Odds are you won't have to explain this unique feature to them.

Common Minor Injuries

Splinters
If you have wood of any sort in your Sugar Glider enclosure, there is a very real chance of it getting splinters. Although, proportionally, the splinter is much larger to a Sugar Glider than it would be to a human being, it usually is not a major emergency for your Sugar Glider. Assuming you have properly bonded with your Sugar Glider, just get a pair of tweezers, find the errant piece of wood and pull it out. Of course, if the splinter should be somewhere sensitive, like the eyes or genital area, you should immediately take it to a veterinarian. If you attempt to remove a splinter from a sensitive area, you run the very real risk of damaging these body structures.

Cuts, bruises and scrapes
Like all pets, Sugar Gliders may sometimes get cuts or bruises, usually from rough housing in their habitat with each other, or they may make an errant glide somewhere and land rougher than they had anticipated. The procedure is pretty simple - keep any wounds clean and dry. If it is very shallow, it will probably take care of itself. Please refrain from putting antibiotic ointment on any wounds, as Sugar Gliders are habitual self-groomers and will certainly consume it. At the very least, this will make your Sugar Glider extremely ill, at worst, it will probably kill your Sugar Glider (or any other Sugar Glider grooming it!). Your veterinarian probably has more suitable Sugar Glider tolerable ointments, please refer to them. If you insist on having the wound cleaned out before taking it to a veterinarian, rinsing it with a simple *sterile* saline solution will do much to help in the interim.

Obviously, for more serious injuries, take your Sugar Glider to the vet. You need to pay attention to how often these minor injuries occur, and to which Sugar Glider in particular it is happening to. If there seems to be one Sugar Glider regularly getting scraped up, chances are pretty decent you may have an issue with another Sugar Glider attempting to establish dominance over it. Be especially aware of injuries around the shoulders or neck of your Sugar Glider- these may be dominance injuries or even mating injuries if your Sugar Glider happens to be female.

Damaged nails
Sugar Gliders can and will damage their nails during the course of their routine habits. The very first thing you should do is to closely inspect the damage- make sure it is just a superficial nail injury and not something more serious like an injured or broken toe. If it is a damaged nail, frankly,

there is not a lot you can do other than let it heal on its own. Of course if it is bleeding, you can apply a styptic powder (such as Kwikstop or Miracle Care), and that should clot up the bleed very quickly. Luckily, Sugar Glider nails grow back very quickly, so any nail injury should heal over quickly. If you have a nail missing entirely, you should probably take your Sugar Glider to the veterinarian just to head off the possibility of an infection setting in.

Common Serious Injuries

As best as you try, sometimes bad things will happen to your Sugar Glider. Most of the time, there are preventative steps you can take to keep something serious from injuring your Sugar Glider. Keeping curious potentially predatory animals and small children far away will greatly extend your Sugar Gliders lifespan. Make sure children are well behaved and closely supervised when allowed contact with your Sugar Gliders- even well intentioned children may mistake your pet for a plush toy and give it a little too hard of a loving squeeze!

Lots of Sugar Glider owners will vehemently disagree with this blanket statement, but it is recommended in the strongest terms possible to not allow contact between your Sugar Gliders and other pets. There is a very low probability for disease transmission, that is true, but there are other variables there you cannot control. First of all, your other pets, like the Sugar Glider are curious. They have very little awareness of their own strength as well. A playful dog or cat will give you a loving swat of the paw- which is no big deal to us large animals, but will feel like Thor's hammer to your poor Sugar Glider. Also, due to the jumpy nature of your furry pet, your Sugar Glider runs the very real risk of startling your other pet.

If your dog or cat does not even seem interested in your Sugar Glider, it may glide on to them, scare them and provoke a fear nip, bite or swat. Although your pet truly meant no harm and was simply reacting to something it was scared of, it could mean game over for your Sugar Glider. If your pet is overly curious about your Sugar Glider, that should come across as a warning sign to keep the two species separated.

Broken Bones in your Sugar Glider
There are two causes of broken bones in Sugar Gliders. By far the most common (and not obvious) cause of broken bones in Sugar Gliders is poor diet. Their skeletons have very specific nutritional needs, and if you are not following the guidelines that have been laid out for you earlier in the book, you run the very serious and real risk of making your Sugar Gliders bones

very brittle. This means that even a normal level of activity from your Sugar Glider, with no extreme forces involved, could very easily break its bones.

The second most common cause of broken bones in Sugar Gliders is from injury. Usually, this means that something is wrong in their habitat. If you have decided to skimp on your Sugar Gliders cage and decided to get them a bird cage with vertical metal bars, you are almost certainly going to cause either a fractured or broken bone in your Sugar Glider. They will not be able to get a firm grasp on the bars and will frequently be seen sliding down them. It is only a matter of time before they try to overcompensate and fly too hard into the bars to assure they land with as proper a grip as they can muster or they slide down and strike something.

Outside of their habitat, playtime in the wider world usually runs the risk of a Sugar Glider injuring itself- although proper supervision can make such play time much safer for your pet. If you see your Sugar Glider ambling for a jump that is simply too far, or on to something dangerous (like a body of water or another pet), stop it!

Symptoms to look for include barking, lameness and lethargy. Sometimes the break will be obvious, like a limb is being dragged around during its movements, sometimes it will be more subtle. Broken ribs or a damaged bone in the spine don't easily manifest themselves, so if you suspect something is wrong or broken on your Sugar Glider, please take it to the veterinarian.

Animal Bites
To be frank, most animal bites will be fatal to your Sugar Glider. It is very rare that an animal will attack another and simply retreat after the first bite. Animals tend to finish what they start, and biting can happen very quickly. Even if you are in the room when an attack on your Sugar Glider begins, by the time you try to break up the incident, several bites may have already landed on your Sugar Gliders delicate frame. If you are not present, chances are very good you will stumble upon a dead Sugar Glider by the time you realized what has happened.

If somehow your Sugar Glider survives an animal bite, please rush it to the veterinarian. Do not waste valuable time trying to ascertain how serious the injury may be. A cat bite to a human being may just be a serious annoyance requiring a little washing out, antibiotic ointment and a bandage. From your Sugar Gliders perspective, however, it has just had several large steak knives driven into it. If you had been stabbed by several large steak knives simultaneously, would you take the time to ascertain if they had hit anything critical, or would you rush to the emergency room and let the experts sort it out for you?

When to see a veterinarian

What veterinarian schedule should my Sugar Glider be on?
Like all pets, Sugar Gliders should be on a routine schedule to visit with your veterinarian. Some veterinarians say you should visit them every six months, some say once a year. To be honest, either schedule is fine, and although the more often, the merrier (it is better to catch problems earlier rather than play catch up); your budget should be taken into account for routine check-ups. Luckily, relative to other pets, Sugar Gliders are relatively low maintenance. There are some guidelines for when you should be concerned and see your veterinarian as soon as possible.

When is it appropriate to worry about your Sugar Glider?
As in pets or children, sometimes it is hard to figure out exactly when something is wrong. Like *all* pets, clear communication is impossible, and you need to watch the animal's behaviour to determine when something is "off" with your pet. Below are some general symptoms to watch out for in your Sugar Gliders.

Symptoms of your Sugar Glider being sick
- Decrease in appetite
- Excessive sleeping
- Diarrhoea
- Decrease in drinking
- Difficult or infrequent bowel movements
- Rash, yellowing or blistering of the skin
- Vomiting
- Excessive urination
- Excessive barking
- Green faeces
- Lameness
- Limping
- Weakness, inability to grip as well
- Paralysis
- Bad breath
- Loss of weight
- Eye discharge
- Self-mutilation
- Seizures
- Convulsions

The above list is a sort of quick guide, if any of the symptoms are spotted, it is imperative you take your Sugar Glider to the veterinarian immediately for proper diagnosis and treatment. Although some of the symptoms may not appear serious to you (like diarrhoea for example), due to the small frame of your Sugar Gliders body, it is an emergency. Some symptoms may be for specific illnesses, and we will discuss this later in the book.

First aid

Preparation is always a good thing, and little emergencies can always come up. Sometimes, having a plan for first aid can help stabilize things until you can get to the veterinarians office for larger medical interventions. Sure, you are thinking you can just throw things together when the time comes up, and perhaps if you have had real world emergency training, you know for a fact you can perform under dire circumstances. Most people, however, mishandle a situation when an emergency comes up. Even if you have the appropriate demeanor, a lack of supplies can make an emergency much worse.

First Aid Kit

Medicine and Food :
- 1 cc oral syringes (useful for medication)
- 3 cc oral syringes (useful for medication, feeding)
- Pedialyte (rehydration)
- Gliderade (rehydration)
- #5 French catheter (for force feeding, if suggested by veterinarian)
- Chicken/mixed vegetable baby food (emergency food supply)
- Small ceramic dish
- Ensure (for mixing with medication/making more palatable)
- Dried fruit (emergency food supply)

For Evacuation and Emergency Travel Purposes :
- Candles (for loss of power)
- Bottled water (for loss of water)
- Fleece blanket (useful for handling in an emergency)
- Emergency contact information (It helps to laminate it. Needs the information of your regular veterinarian, emergency all night veterinarians and the animal poison line for your region)
- A copy of the Sugar Gliders medical records
- Ready to go travel cage (so you can put your Sugar Glider in quickly and transport it)
- Flashlight

For Sanitation Purposes :
- Hand sanitizer
- Alcohol wipes
- Rubber gloves
- Paper towels

Injury Care :
- Tri-tops antibiotic ointment (veterinarian prescribed)
- Baby Anbesol (used for tooth pain, contains benzocaine, useful for emergency pain relief)
- Sterile saline solution (for cleaning out wounds)
- Q-tips
- Toothpicks (to make an impromptu splint)
- Iodine swab stick (also for cleaning out wounds)
- 22 and 25 gauge needles
- 3cc and 10cc sterile syringes

Miscellaneous :
- Cash (if you need to buy something in a pinch, or for being able to pay your veterinarian in an emergency situation where credit card processing systems may or not be functioning)
- Styptic powder (to stem bleeding)
- Tweezers (splinters happen)
- Digital scale (keep track of your Sugar Gliders weight, especially if placed on a diet)
- Small scissors (if your Sugar Glider should happen to get really wrapped up in threading, you can quickly break them out)
- Non-alcohol wipes (baby wipes, you can never have enough)
- Disposable ice pack (for sudden travel in hot weather)
- Heat pack/hand warmer (for sudden travel in cold weather)
- Emergency supply checklist

The above sounds like a lot of stuff, but frankly, most of it can probably fit into a child's lunch box. Certain things are optional- for example, if you live in a tropical climate, you can probably skip purchasing emergency sources of warmth. Review the list and use your own good judgement, and don't forget to ask your veterinarian for suggestions as well.

Breeding sugar gliders

To reiterate a common theme through this book- there are many unwanted and homeless Sugar Gliders in the world. There is already an excess supply of Sugar Gliders in need of loving homes. Please refrain from breeding Sugar Gliders unless you know *exactly* what you are doing. If you happen to live in a remote area where adopting or purchasing additional Sugar

Gliders happens to be extremely difficult and you know exactly who is going to house and care for them, then by all means, aid in making more Sugar Gliders. If you simply want to breed them because it is cute to do so, please refrain from doing so. Every Sugar Glider is a life, and they are quite a commitment compared to other small mammals.

Each Sugar Glider can live up to 15 years! 80% of litters are twins, and in captivity, Sugar Gliders can breed year round. If you happen to have a colony of Sugar Gliders instead of just a pair, multiply the math of the above. If you don't know what you are doing, you can end up with more joeys than you bargained for, then what? Please don't make animals suffer because of your lack of adequate planning.

The Details

Legal Issues
Please double check to make sure that breeding of Sugar Gliders is even permissible where you live. Just because your jurisdiction permits the *ownership* of Sugar Gliders doesn't necessarily mean you are permitted to *breed* Sugar Gliders. For example, in some states in the United States, you need to have a USDA license to breed Sugar Gliders (above a certain number bred usually means you need a commercial license). Some jurisdictions prohibit their breeding by private collectors all together. Please make sure you have cleared any legal or regulatory hurdles before you set about making joeys. It would be difficult to be fined, and very sad to have animals seized should the authorities find out you have been improperly breeding your Sugar Gliders.

Male Sexual Behavior
As in most species of mammals, males will need no prompting to engage in sex. In their natural habitat, males are polygynous, meaning usually one (maybe even up to two) of the oldest males' rules over a harem of several females. The only way fertile males will tolerate each other's presence is if they are closely related (siblings or a father and son pair). All other males are driven away, in a vicious fashion usually. In captivity however, usually only one fertile male will be active, and if you insist on keeping multiple fertile males, please keep a close eye on them for hostile behavior. The fertile males *must* be closely related, or fighting *will happen*. There will be no gentleman's agreement amongst your male Sugar Gliders.

There are external signs that you should be aware of, indicating that your male Sugar Glider is reaching sexual maturity. Just as in human sexual maturation, these signs become more pronounced as they get older. First is age- males hit sexual maturity at 12 to 14 months. As they get older, you will notice a change in their scent gland areas (especially the gland on the head). It will be very subtle at first and hard to notice, but as time goes on, you will start noticing the production of waxy glandular products and mild hair loss. When maturation is advanced, baldness will strike the gland area (or areas, depending on the virility of your individual Sugar Glider); especially the gland on the head. You will notice the fur in the vicinity of the gland areas becoming discolored due to the secretions of the glands.

The genitalia will change as well. The testicle sac will usually become larger. You will notice more frequent erections as well. Like most young males, grooming and masturbation may be witnessed- this is perfectly normal. You can choose to call it either one, I suppose it is only a matter of degree. Some have euphemistically dubbed the behavior as "flossing", I will leave it to your imagination as to why is has received that name. Excessive "grooming" may be a cause for concern as it may indicate the presence of an injury or infection. If your male Sugar Glider seems pathologically entranced with its genitals, you may want to take it to your veterinarian to rule out any injuries or disease.

Female Sexual Behavior
In the wild, Sugar Gliders breed only during the cooler months of June to November (since Australia is in the Southern Hemisphere and has seasons the opposite time of year to their Northern Hemispheric friends). It is thought that the seasonal breeding of Sugar Gliders is linked to the availability of insect protein during this season. This would explain why in the further reaches of Northern Australia (and the island of New Guinea), where insects are not as affected by the milder change in seasons as their further south counterparts, Sugar Glider breeding can occur year round.

Like human beings, female Sugar Gliders are polyestrous, meaning they are continually capable of becoming pregnant. The fertility cycle is strikingly similar in length of time to that of a human being as well- they have a 29 day cycle. In captivity and in tropical habitats, females can breed year round.

Fate of the Young
In their natural habitat, Sugar Glider joeys initially only weigh 0.2 grams (almost nothing in terms of ounces) when they are first born- a little less than the weight of a single grain of rice! Birth weight in captivity is the same. Most are born with a sibling (80%) - though not necessarily a twin. Due to the bifurcated anatomy of female Sugar Gliders, it is usually two separate egg and ova that have combined to make two unique Sugar Gliders. Gestation period is 15 to 17 days; the fetus crawls into the

mother's marsupium and remains there for a further 70 to 74 days. Once they outgrow their mothers pouch, they are left in the nest to grow more until they are aged 110 to 120 days, after which they will further participate in colony life. The young are then forcibly dispersed by the colony at 7 to 10 months of age. This is probably done to limit the competition for resources and prevent any sort of inbreeding from occurring, as is practiced in many species.

Get down to business

Prompting sexual behavior
Sugar Gliders, as most mammalian pets, will not need a ton of prompting to engage in sexual behavior. It really is as simple as having a fertile male (aged 12 to 15 months or older in males, 8 to 12 months of age in females) in proximity to each other, and it will happen. Lust is in their nature as much as it is in ours.

Genetics
If you have a certain "look" in mind for the Sugar Gliders you wish to conjure up, you have to have at least a basic understanding of the science of genetics. It is not hard to learn about, I swear. There are some common sense rules of thumb to understand first before you engage in breeding Sugar Gliders. Most importantly, avoid inbreeding at all costs. The more inbreeding that occurs in a population, the higher the likelihood of there being miscarriages, severe birth defects or disease afflicting the baby joey. Please have thorough documentation for all your Sugar Gliders bloodlines if you intend to breed them. A reputable breeder should have information about the precise ancestry of your Sugar Gliders and can give you more detailed information about how to breed your Sugar Gliders. You want to keep the coeffeciency of interrelatedness as close to 0 as possible (this is a mathematical ratio showing what fraction of genes are shared between two organisms that have a common ancestor in the past). A zero coeffeciency is impossible as all life on Earth is interrelated (insofar as we know).

As in humans, Sugar Gliders have two *types* of chromosomes. These are respectively called autosomes and allosomes. Autosomes are known as the sex chromosomes, and determine the biological gender (and all the specific features this entails) of an organism. Allosomes are the rest of the chromosomes. As in human beings, Sugar Gliders have an XX (female) and XY (male) scheme to determining the gender of their offspring (not all advanced organisms follow this pattern, but that is outside the scope of this book). The only notable difference in structure in the autosome of Sugar Gliders is that the Y chromosome appears even shorter than that of placental animals (ask any geneticist and they will tell you the Y chromosome is already pretty short in such organisms, like ourselves). Anyway, as you may very well remember from high school biology, every gene you have in your body comes either your mother or your father. Half your genes exactly (more or less, again, the precise details are outside the scope of this book) are from your mother or father - but that does not mean they are expressed in an equal fashion. There is the phenomenon of dominant and recessive alleles (which is just a fancy term of the section of DNA that expresses the gene) - you get one allele from mom and one allele from dad. If you pair a dominant to a recessive allele, whatever feature the dominant gene programs for will be expressed (the recessive allele will be "silenced"). If two genes are dominant, clearly the dominant trait is the only that will be expressed. It is only when you have two recessive alleles that a recessive trait can be expressed. Not all recessive traits are bad (you having 5 fingers instead of 6 is a recessive trait, for example), but it is recessive alleles that makes inbreeding so dangerous.

You see, if a dominant gene were devastating or lethal to an organism, it would be selected out very quickly, as it will always be expressed. So any mutation that causes a devastating or lethal dominant allele to arise in an organism almost never gets passed on. If such a mutation occurs in a recessive allele however, it may slip by unnoticed for generations. It will only be expressed when it encounters another recessive allele that it will be expressed. Fun fact: Almost every human being has a lethal recessive allele somewhere in their genome. The same is true for most organisms, and thankfully, they are rarely expressed, due to low rates of inbreeding for human beings and healthy wild populations of organisms. However, the more closely related the population, the higher the likelihood these dangerous recessive alleles will pair up and devastate a new life.

An organism with two of the same alleles, whether or not they are either dominant or recessive is homozygous for that allele. An organism that has two different alleles is called heterozygous. It seems like a mouthful, I understand, but the Latin prefix homo (same) and hetero (different) will help you remember which is which. A useful tool for determining the likelihood of a trait being expressed is the Punnett Square.

Homozygous Punnet Square

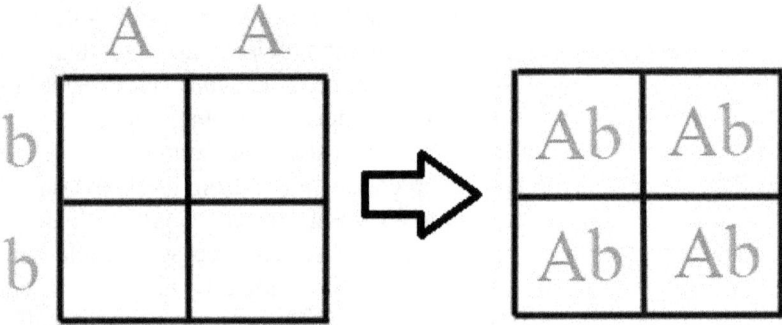

So let's say that "A" programs an organism for green fur while "b" programs for orange fur. Uppercase stands for a dominant allele, while lower case stands for a recessive allele. Both parents in this scenario are homozygous (either pure green or orange fur from an allelic standpoint). All the offspring will have green fur. Even though all the offspring in question will carry an allele for orange fur, all the offspring will have this trait "silenced" by the presence of the dominant green fur allele in their genome.

Homozygous Dominant cross Heterozygous Punnett Square

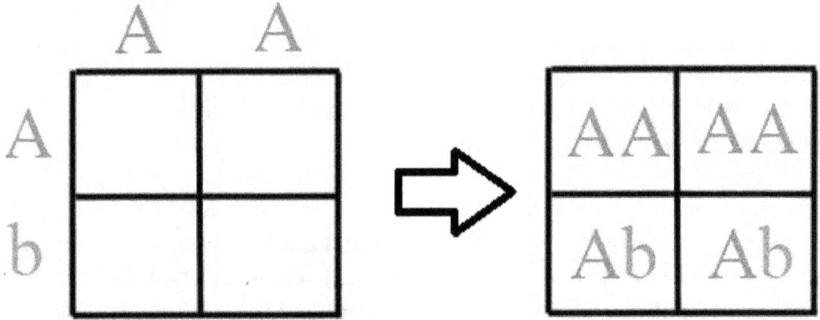

In this example, a pure homozygous dominant parent is cross bred with a heterozygous parent. All the offspring will exhibit green fur, and in fact, in half of the offspring, the allele for expressing orange fur is eliminated from their genome entirely. Only half the offspring will carry the allele for expressing orange fur. So, in genetic terms, half the offspring will be homozygous for green fur, half of them will be heterozygous for green fur.

Homozygous Recessive cross Heterozygous Punnett Square

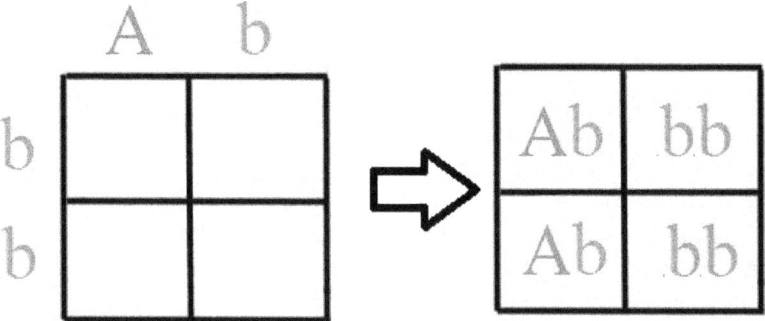

This is the example where the recessive allele (in our case, pure orange fur) will be expressed in the highest proportion of offspring. Wholly 50% of offspring will be homozygous recessive for the orange fur allele, meaning they will actually appear orange. The green fur trait is entirely missing from their genome. Another 50% of the offspring will be heterozygous for the dominant green fur allele, meaning they will have green fur. 100% of the offspring in this scenario will carry at least 1 allele for the orange fur.

Heterozygous crossed with Heterozygous Punnett Square

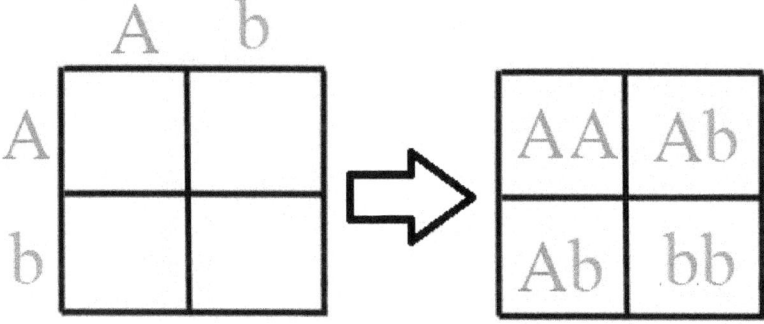

This Punnett Square shows what happens when you cross two heterozygous parents. 75% of the offspring will show the dominant trait (green fur), while only 25% of the offspring will show the recessive trait (orange fur). 75% of the offspring, however, will be carriers of the recessive orange fur allele.

Now that we have condensed a semester of college genetics into a page or so, what does all this have to do with your Sugar Glider? *Certain Sugar Glider morphs happen to follow the above genetic protocols when it comes to their appearance.* The exact term for the inheritance pattern explained above is deemed "Mendelian", named after Gregor Mendel, an early pioneer into genetics famous for his work with peas.

For example, the leucistic Sugar Glider (all white fur and black eyes) has a single recessive allele that causes its unique appearance. Therefore, if you wanted to breed additional leucistic morph Sugar Gliders, you would first have to verify the pedigree of the two Sugar Gliders you wish to breed. If you know for a fact that one parent is a heterozygous leucistic Sugar Glider (which can be guaranteed if you know if 50% of its siblings were leucistic) and you have a leucistic Sugar Glider you want to breed it with, you can guarantee that 50% of your joeys will be leucistic in phenotype (the scientific word for appearance caused by genetic disposition). Even the normal appearing heterozygous Sugar Gliders produced will be more valuable, as you can sell or trade it as a carrier of a relatively valuable allele.

The mosaic Sugar Glider morph (patches of fur that appear inverted in color) is actually a codominant trait- not recessive. However, for our layman's purposes, it may be treated as a recessive gene (we would have to go into the weeds again about genetic minutiae) - there are no heterozygous mosaic Sugar Glider morphs, they have to be homozygous. This means if you have two heterozygous parents for the mosaic morph, you can expect 25% of the joeys to express this phenotype. If you have a heterozygous parent and a homozygous parent, 50% of the joeys will exhibit the mosaic morph features, etcetera, and etcetera. The albino Sugar Glider morph is a recessive trait and follows the same Mendelian pattern of inheritance.

Genetics, as with many other subjects in life sciences, isn't always so straightforward however. There are Sugar Glider morphs that *don't* follow Mendelian patterns of inheritance- usually because the appearance is the effect of *several* alleles interacting. We won't get into the genetics of non-Mendelian inheritance, as its results are far more variable in practice and its theories are far more voluminous than can be comfortably summarized in this book.

Sugar Glider morphs that seem to follow non-Mendelian inheritance patterns include the White Face Blonde, the White Tip, any Sugar Glider Morph described as being red, and frankly any other of the other morphs. This does not mean they all follow the same pattern of breeding to achieve these results, it is just that they do not follow the simple Mendelian pattern explained above (for example, the White Tip morph is caused by multiple recessive genes it seems).

Young sugar gliders
As with all pets, the youngest will have unique needs and present unique challenges to you as the owner. As with most small mammals, please refrain from handling the youngest joeys- there is much anecdotal evidence that this will cause a transfer of your scent to the joey. This increases the chance of fetal rejection, or may even prompt the mother to cannibalize its young! If you *must* handle the youngest joeys (usually due to concern with the mother's health), please leave it to your veterinarian. Joeys may be safely handled when they are old enough to leave the mothers pouch and explore their habitat. Best just to ensure the mother is in good health, and receiving a proper healthy diet.

Understanding their minds
The joeys are the children of your Sugar Glider colony. They have key cognitive milestones, just like young of any other species. They start out life as small as a grain of rice and take about 70 to 74 days to be safely handled by human beings. The mother has a scent gland in her marsupium (pouch) which the fetus finds instinctually attractive; this is how they know where to crawl during their birth. By day 74 (not coincidentally around the time they start leaving the pouch regularly) they can distinguish the scent of their mother from other mother Sugar Gliders in their own colony. By day 94 they can tell their own colony's scent apart from that of another colony.

Hand Raising a Sugar Glider Joey

Why would you hand raise a Joey?
Sometimes life throws a curveball, this is as true for Sugar Gliders as it is for anyone else. Sometimes a mother will die while raising its joeys; sometimes the mother may get an infection in her marsupium (pouch), or even more callously, outright reject the joey. Rejection most often occurs when the mother detects a birth deformity. Frankly, depending on how young the joey is, it is very difficult to successfully hand read a marsupial joey, simply because they are all born "premature" compared to placental mammal babies. They will need a tremendous amount of work to successfully bring up.

Generally, the older the joey is at the stage of rejection, the easier it is to raise. Unfortunately, most joeys (that are rejected at all, which is the extreme minority) are rejected within the first two weeks of their crawling into the marsupium. These are all valid reasons for hand raising a joey. A joey should *never* be separated from its mother simply because you want to, or you think it will make it easier to handle later on in life. This is extremely cruel, and frankly, you will never do as good a job as the mother naturally could. It should be a last resort, a last ditch effort to spare the life of a joey that would die otherwise without your intervention.

Common Signs of Rejection
- Joey is left alone in nest for more than 15 minutes by both parents
- Joey cries and parents fail to respond
- Joey attempts to leave the nest (before 4 to 5 weeks out of the pouch)
- Joey is found alone on the cage bottom
- Joey shows signs of injury (bites, scratches, mutilation of any sort)
- Joey is found dehydrated

You can't eyeball if a Joey is dehydrated. To check for joey dehydration, you need to lift the skin (gently) off the shoulder blades. It should be supple and immediately pull back to its original form. If it stays pinched up or takes a long time to resume its form over the joey's shoulders, your joey is dehydrated. Once you have determined that your joey is dehydrated, you need to feed it (well, water it, I suppose) unflavored Pedialyte for the first 24 hours to make up for the mothers neglect.

You can also rule out an accidental fall out of the nest. Although, if you have equipped your habitat appropriately, it should be *very* difficult for the joey to escape, but never underestimate the resolve of baby animals! Accidents do happen. If you find a joey at the bottom of your habitat, you need to place the joey on the *father's* back. He (should) instinctually start to carry the joey back into the nest where he will help clean it up for the mother. If he drops the joey or otherwise ignores it, it means your joey is rejected. You may try to rehydrate the joey and keep it warm for an hour or so and repeat the process. Also understand that a cold joey will not drink- warm it up first!

Please stay nearby during reintroduction attempts- if the parents are hostile they may try to injure or kill the joey. Even if they just abandon it, if you are away for too long it could die of hypothermia or dehydration before you come back. If the parents still continue to neglect the joey, it definitively means it is abandoned and you will have to hand raise it.

What to Expect
Joeys are born hairless- by the time of rejection (or other form of orphanage) they may still have very little or no hair. To be honest, they are quite ugly during their youngest years. The first order of business is to ensure your joey stays warm, round the clock. Cloacal temperature (the cloaca probably being most similar to the marsupium in terms of structure) of Sugar Gliders is 89 degrees Fahrenheit (31.6 C), with rectal temperature

readings usually being about 97 degrees Fahrenheit (36.1 C)- you should strive to keep your joey *somewhat below this temperature range* with a heating pad, of course with some insulation. Remember, when you were suckling at your mothers bosom, it was on her exterior, so your swaddled form was not coddled at 98.6 degrees Fahrenheit (37 C)- you would have not been able to lose excess heat and would have died if you were kept at that temperature.

Likewise, your joey is a mammal that needs to bleed off some of its excess heat. The *ideal temperature range for your joey is between 80 and 85 degrees Fahrenheit (26.6 C and 29.4 C)*. There is a lot of debate about whether or not a heating rock is appropriate for a joey due to its limited mobility. Frankly, I would defer to the advice of my veterinarian on this topic. If you should choose to use a heating rock, *do not put the joey directly onto the rock. Please insulate it with a shirt or towel.* Due to the small volume of their bodies, joeys can become hypothermic at room temperature in a matter of minutes.

You will need to feed your orphaned joey. Luckily they will only need to eat 3 or 4 times a day. They do have very special dietary needs, however. You cannot get away with feeding your joeys cow (or goat, etc.) milk and some multivitamin and call it a day. Remember we exhaustively covered how large the evolutionary gaps between placental mammals and marsupials earlier in this book- you are way more similar to a cow (genetically and nutritionally) than to a Sugar Glider.

You will need to order a marsupial milk replacer- by far the most popular brand is Wombaroo Sugar Glider Milk Replacer. It is made in Australia (where there are tons of marsupials in need of help from the local wildlife managers) specifically for weening marsupials.

You will also need to buy Impact Colostrum Supplement. Those of you who are mothers to your own children may be familiar with the term colostrum. In placental mammals, it is the milk that is usually produced during the earliest periods of lactation after birth. This milk is very high in protein content and also contains a large amount of antibodies - basically this is the milk that helps to rapidly build the immune systems of placental mammal young.

After a few days, more typical milk (higher in fat and lower in protein) is produced for the duration of lactation. Marsupials however *do not have* an analogous colostrum period milk. So why is it so important that we provide this supplement to orphaned joeys? Because *all* the milk marsupials produce has *colostrum like properties* (i.e. it is generally higher in protein and much higher in antibodies than placental mammal milk) for the duration of lactation.

Old sugar gliders

Sugar Gliders get older. Who doesn't? Usually you will notice your Sugar Glider approaching its golden years at around the 9 year mark. The patterns of aging for Sugar Gliders are remarkably similar to that of human beings- the physical and mental changes have a striking parallel. Generally, aging has symptoms affecting behavior, weight, fur pattern and diet.

Behavioral Changes in your Aging Sugar Glider

You will notice some habits shift - for example, if your Sugar Glider was never active during daylight hours, this may change. We all know our sleeping patterns change as we get older - it is more or less the same thing for your pet Sugar Glider. This is analogous to senior citizens roaming around the house at night- especially in search of a snack. Of course, as age takes its toll on the muscles, bones and joints of your Sugar Glider, you will notice they will become less active with age. This is perfectly normal.

You will notice a decline in their agility and mobility; this is usually symptomatic of arthritis. If you happen to find your Sugar Glider sleeping alone (which is very unusual for such social animals), in an unusual spot (on the floor cage, exercise wheel, etc.), this may be a sign of deep distress on the part of your Sugar Glider. Please take your aging Sugar Glider to your veterinarian in this instance.

Change in Eating and Drinking habits

Your Sugar Gliders appetite should remain steady and healthy as it ages. Some may even put on a little weight, depending on their activity levels. However, moderate loss in weight is perfectly normal as well; it is just your Sugar Gliders body aging. Your Sugar Glider should not be easily showing any skeletal bones (ribs, shoulder blades, etc.) so if your Sugar Glider is appearing particularly gaunt, please take it to the veterinarian as soon as possible, as this is probably a clear indication of a larger medical issue going on with your pet Sugar Glider.

You will also notice that your older Sugar Gliders will actually appear thirstier- they will drink more water than younger Sugar Gliders. Some veterinarians speculate that this is because of reduced kidney function, or may be symptomatic of a diabetic problem. If you suspect your animal may be having issues with kidney function or diabetes, there are tests that can be performed by your veterinarian, if they happen to suggest such an intervention is necessary.

Change in your Sugar Gliders appearance
Your Sugar Glider will lose a moderate amount of weight as it ages (read the above section on eating habits). You should only be concerned when the weight loss is anything more than moderate. Your Sugar Gliders fur coat will also suffer with age. The most substantial thinning of fur on your Sugar Glider will occur on its tail. Your males are already somewhat bald from their puberty phase.

Hair color will not change with age as in humans (Sugar Gliders already start off grey, for the most part!), but you may notice your Sugar Gliders fur will look a little "worn", it will definitely lose luster with age.

Chapter 11. Diseases that afflict your Sugar Glider

It should be said that if your Sugar Glider appears to be deathly ill, please do not hesitate to take it to the veterinarian. This book should only be used as a handy prevention guide - not a cure all. Always take your Sugar Glider in for a real, honest to goodness physical inspection by a professional, even if you are 100% sure of what ails your Sugar Glider. There are sometimes variables that are subtle to see, or cannot be tested for in a home setting. Understand that symptoms of many different diseases are often very similar to one another - the body (in this case, your Sugar Glider's body) only has so many ways to defend itself! Do not gamble with your Sugar Glider's life.

Common Ailments
This will be a sort of "greatest hits" list of what most commonly ails your Sugar Glider. Please do not ignore the possibility of rarer ailments- just because a disease is rare does not mean it is impossible! Cancers and such do occur in Sugar Gliders, usually towards the end of their lives. Unfortunately due to their small size and relatively fragile, the more drastic the disease the more likely your Sugar Glider will die. Be grateful if your Sugar Glider makes it to old age however, because a few simple mistakes will drastically shorten your Sugar Gliders lifespan. Please take the time to adequately review basic safety tips and dietary requirements for your Sugar Glider. If you do so, most of the ailments described below can easily be prevented and avoided altogether.

Psychological Ailments
Sugar Gliders are socially complex and relatively intelligent animals. As such, they will have psychological issues crop up more frequently than would appear in simpler animals (say, reptiles). Due to their unique social needs and sensitivity to hierarchy, you must keep a watchful eye on their psychological well-being.

Depression
Symptoms of depression in Sugar Gliders are remarkably similar to the symptoms found in humans. Indeed, Sugar Gliders are often used as model animals in laboratories studying human depression. Symptoms include lethargic behavior, low energy levels, withdrawal from social interaction and heightened irritability. Everyone (including your pet Sugar Glider) can have a bad day every once in a while, but if you notice persistent behaviors

including the above combined with lack of sleep (in your Sugar Gliders case, unusual activity during daylight hours) and loss of appetite for a prolonged period of time, you should be concerned.

Often times, depression in Sugar Gliders is brought on by understandable circumstances. For example, if a close companion animal to your Sugar Glider has recently died, depression is quite common. However, sometimes depression can be cause by illness, isolation or perceived neglect (you are not interacting with it enough). If you suspect your Sugar Glider has come down with the case of the blues, please take it to your veterinarian for a proper diagnosis. This will rule out more serious ailments and potentially head off more serious changes in behavior (such as self-mutilation). Prevention is key, so please remember to house your Sugar Glider with other Sugar Gliders, provide plenty of treats and toys and interact with it frequently, and you should be fine.

Stress
What on Earth could a Sugar Glider be stressed out about? Quite a bit actually. Common things that add to the stress in a Sugar Glider's life include loneliness, illness, inadequate diet and disrupted sleep. Try to only handle your Sugar Gliders minimally during daylight hours- imagine how stressed you would be if a giant came along every single evening to wake you to play for a few hours before morning came along. Also perceived dangers can make your pet Sugar Glider stressed as well.

For example, if you have a curious cat in the house and it consistently stalks your Sugar Glider outside of its cage, this is pretty stressful from the Sugar Gliders perspective. You have to understand it doesn't know it is perfectly safe inside of its cage. Sudden changes in environment are also stressful- animals tend to be pretty conservative about where they live.

Also hormonal issues involving the thyroid gland may stress your Sugar Glider out. Stress is bad, and although unavoidable at times, please keep your Sugar Gliders as stress free as possible. If your pet Sugar Glider should happen to live under chronic stress, its health and mental wellbeing will deteriorate. Symptoms of stress closely mirror those of depression.

Self-Mutilation
This is an extremely unfortunate outcome. This malignant behavior is most often expressed in solitary Sugar Gliders. Sugar Gliders should never be kept alone- they will devolve into a psychologically disturbed state. Stressed Sugar Gliders likewise will often turn to self-mutilation as a form of relief. The symptoms are pretty obvious, and include chewing injuries to the tail, limbs, penis and scrotum. Stressors that often lead to depression, if

left neglected long enough, will turn into self-mutilation. First thing you should do if meet with your veterinarian for general injury care. Your veterinarian should clean out the wounds and make a modified Elizabethan collar to keep your Sugar Glider from further injuring itself while it physically heals. You should then review what state of affairs led to your Sugar Gliders drastic behavior. Often time, poor nutrition or sleep is to blame, if the social setting is normal.

If everything is right in the Sugar Gliders world and you are at a loss for what is prompting this behavior, you may need to have the hard talk with your veterinarian about administering antidepressant medication to your Sugar Glider. SSRI's (selective serotonin reuptake inhibitors) like fluoxetine or paroxetine are usually used for correcting what is euphemistically dubbed as "stereotypic behavior" in animals. Recommended first line of treatment (if SSRI's are decided upon) is .5 to 1 mg/kg by mouth of fluoxetine. Again, please meet with your veterinarian before deciding upon a course of action, and never ever give your Sugar Glider any medication that is intended, packaged and sold for human consumption.

A postulated alternate cause of self-mutilation behavior is pain. Some perfectly healthy Sugar Gliders have been known to engage in self-mutilation after surgery, usually attacking wherever they have been operated on. It is thought that the painkillers used during the procedure wear off, and for lack of a better alternative, the Sugar Glider will mutilate the area to increase release of pain inhibiting endorphins. Please discuss this possibility with your veterinarian if you know your Sugar Glider is going to have a scheduled surgical procedure.

Teeth Problems
As stated in earlier chapters, Sugar Gliders belong to the family of marsupials called diprotodonts, meaning they have prominent mandibular central incisors (i.e. the two middle teeth in the lower jaw are prominently longer than the other teeth). Sugar Gliders are believed to have specialized these teeth into fruit and bark scraping roles in their natural wild behavior. These teeth are permanent, thus they never ever need to be trimmed, and in fact, if you attempt to do so you will cause your Sugar Glider great pain and greatly increase their chances of having an infected tooth. If this happens, the tooth (or teeth) will need to be extracted.

The diet of Sugar Gliders is particularly hard on their teeth. They eat a lot of carbohydrates (fruits and such), so tartar buildup is all but inevitable. Feeding your Sugar Gliders insects with hard exoskeletons will help mitigate tartar buildup on their teeth. Periodontitis is also possible with your Sugar Glider. If you notice your Sugar Glider eating less, or eating more gingerly this may indicate issues with their teeth.

If your Sugar Glider is unfortunate enough to experience a tooth extraction, there are things you could do as the owner to speed recovery. Besides whatever medications your veterinarian prescribes you, you can also help keep the extraction site clean. Note that not all Sugar Gliders will permit this, but some lucky owners have reported success cleaning the tooth extraction site by putting a child friendly fruit flavored antiseptic mouthwash on a cotton swab, and gently cleaning the area. Your mileage will vary, depending on how cooperative your particular pet Sugar Glider is. As always, preventative care is best, please make sure your Sugar Glider has a proper well rounded diet.

Malnutrition
Rather than going into excruciating detail about what needs to be in their diet and in what proportion, we will only discuss the symptoms and types of malnutrition pet Sugar Gliders most often suffer from. Please review the chapters on how and what to feed your pet Sugar Gliders.

Differing Forms of Malnutrition
- Hypoproteinemia- Caused by a lack of protein in the diet. This is extremely bad for the muscles and organs of your Sugar Glider. Surely you have seen the pictures of starving children in the Global South with extended bellies? This is caused by nutritional hypoproteinemia. Your Sugar Glider will have abnormal bloodwork results and be extremely lethargic. Anemia is probably comorbid with the hypoproteinemia, the various mucus membranes (gums, etc.) will have a pallor to them and bruising will more than likely be apparent. Your Sugar Glider will be far more susceptible to infections.

- Hypocalcaemia- This is caused by a lack of calcium in the diet. Your Sugar Glider will be thin and dehydrated. Seizures may be possible, and bone fractures are far more likely. If your Sugar Gliders spinal column should break because of a lack of calcium in its diet, it may become paralyzed.

- Hypoglycemia- Low blood sugar. This is found when diabetes is present- take your Sugar Glider to the veterinarian immediately for treatment, they may die very quickly. Symptoms include clumsiness, confusion, seizures and unconsciousness.

- Hypovitaminosis B_1- The vitamin B1 (also known as Thiamine) is critically important to your Sugar Glider. This form of malnutrition is also common known as Thiamine deficiency. Symptoms include an overly fast heart rate, muscle weakness and shortness of breath.

Gastrointestinal Issues

Diarrhea and vomiting

Due to your Sugar Gliders small body volume, waste no time pondering if this is serious. It is. Your Sugar Glider can become critically dehydrated in a matter of a few hours, immediately take your Sugar Glider to the veterinarian. If you are reading his section because your pet is having these issues, drop the book and head out with your critically ill pet!

If you are reading simply as an academic exercise, or in preparation for life with your Sugar Glider however, continue reading on. Most of the time diarrhea is indicative of enteritis (inflammation of the small intestine) or enteropathy (disease of the small intestine). This is usually caused by the presence of a bacterial or protozoan pathogen. The usual suspects, respectively are *Escherichia Coli* or *Giardia*. Other causes include malnutrition, a metabolic disorder (an issue with either kidney or liver function) or even simple stress. Diagnosis usually requires fecal analysis, a complete blood count, the collection of bacterial cultures and fecal Gram's stains.

Constipation

Basically the same in Sugar Gliders as it is in human beings. If your Sugar Glider appears to be having a hard time passing waste, it is probably constipated. Usually, they will show distress by barking while defecating. It is usually caused by lack of fiber, dehydration, lack of exercise, stress or poor diet. Certain medications may also contribute. Baby food prunes and a little bit of mineral oil is fine for minor cases of constipation - but still, take your Sugar Glider to the vet if you suspect something major. If the case is serious enough, your Sugar Glider may die from the back up.

Rectal/Cloacal Prolapse

This is as painful as it looks. When either the rectum or cloaca prolapses (that is, slides such that it looks like either the rectum or cloaca is attempting to turn itself inside out), head to the veterinarian immediately. Only surgical intervention can help.

Intestinal Blockage

It is exactly what is sounds like - something has gotten stuck in your Sugar Glider's intestines. Usually this is the result of some inedible part of its food being swallowed. For example, a whole seed is swallowed, or a husk is consumed. This is why you must exercise caution as to what treats you will feed your Sugar Gliders - nuts are particularly notorious for causing intestinal blockages. Symptoms will include abdominal bloating or swelling, vomiting and complete inability to pass feces. Sometimes partial blockages will permit diarrhea to pass through. There is nothing for you to do other than rush your Sugar Glider to your veterinarian. Only surgery can save your Sugar Gliders life in this instance.

Aflatoxicosis

This is a form of poisoning that may afflict your Sugar Glider. It is caused by your Sugar Glider coming into contact with eating corn, cottonseed peanuts or insects that contain aflatoxins. Aflatoxins are metabolic byproducts produced by fungi (like mold). Sometimes corn or cottonseed isn't stored properly and they may develop small mold colonies (feeder insects are sometimes fed with contaminated grain, this is how they come to contain aflatoxins). Long term effects of aflatoxin exposure can include cancer. Acute aflatoxicosis can kill in a matter of hours, so please rush your Sugar Glider to the veterinarian if you suspect it has been poisoned with aflatoxins. Symptoms include loss of energy, diarrhea, decreased appetite and jaundice (yellowing of skin and mucus membranes).

Giardiasis

As the name would suggest, Giardiasis is caused by the parasite protozoan *Giardia lamblia*. A protozoan is a single cell microscopic eukaryote, not a bacteria (which is a prokaryote). It is an extremely common cause of waterborne disease. It usually blooms in the small intestines of pet Sugar Gliders and can be very dangerous, since its principle symptom is an immense amount of diarrhea. Human beings are susceptible to infection from Giardia, so exercise caution if you suspect your Sugar Gliders stool might contain the parasite (although it isn't nearly so dangerous for human beings, it would be a tremendous annoyance).

Sugar Gliders most often contract Giardia through contaminated water or by coming into contact with an infected animal (and thus, its feces). Other symptoms include lameness, jaundice, vomiting and dehydration. If you suspect your Sugar Glider is contaminated with Giardia, please isolate it from other Sugar Gliders in your colonies as quickly as possible to keep it from spreading. You will also need to sterilize the habitat that your Sugar Gliders live in to reduce the chance of transmission to them.

Lumpy Jaw

Lumpy jaw, as it is called, is actually the result of a bacterial infection. The exact species responsible for this disease is *Actinomyces israeli,* and as the name suggests, the disease most often occurs on the face (the jaw area). It is a slowly growing lump that will get larger, and if left untreated, the infection may spread to the lungs, intestines and other sensitive regions of the body. Ultimately, the disease is fatal if left untreated, much like any other major bacterial infection. The most common point of entry for this disease is a dental abscess in your Sugar Gliders jaw, so please pay special attention to your pet Sugar Gliders dental needs. Symptoms include a lump forming on the face, chest or neck, weight loss and eye discharge. Usually your veterinarian will prescribe the appropriate antibiotics to resolves this infection.

Trichomoniasis
Trichomoniasis is another disease caused by a pesky protozoan. Although primarily a gynecological concern for human beings (being spread primarily by sexual contact), in your Sugar Glider it most often presents itself far more subtly. The only symptoms are weight loss and vomiting. Sugar Gliders usually contract this disease by coming into contact with a contaminated water or food supply. Always ensure your Sugar Glider is drinking bottled spring water, and wash your hands thoroughly before handling its food. A quick trip to the veterinarian will resolve this disease.

Hind leg paralysis
This is an affliction actually named for the primary symptom! If your Sugar Gliders back two legs appear to be paralyzed, it is probably suffering from nutritional secondary hyperparathyroidism. Unlike a spinal injury, this form of paralysis is reversible if caught early enough. Basically, your Sugar Glider isn't receiving proper nutrition, so its thyroid glands are pumping out excess parathyroid hormone.

This hormone leaches calcium from its skeleton- leading to the neurological imbalance that expresses itself as hind leg paralysis. Other symptoms to watch out for include poor gripping ability, tremors, limping and weakness. Again, this is perfectly preventable with proper nutrition and reversible if taken to the veterinarian who will undoubtedly administer medication and dietary suggestions.

Ear Margin Canker
Basically, this is a crusting of the ear or ears of your Sugar Glider and will present an irregular shape. It is most often caused by an ear mite infestation. Your veterinarian will probably prescribe ivermectin and topical antibiotics. Occasionally, ear margin canker may be the result of abuse from another Sugar Glider (biting leading to infected ears), ergot poisoning (eating moldy grains) or frostbite. Never expose your Sugar Glider to extreme cold, please.

Eye Problems

I'm sure you have noticed your Sugar Glider has large protruding eyes. As cute as they are, they are nonetheless a liability. Corneal scratches (comorbid with conjunctivitis and ulceration) are caused mostly by scratches inflicted by cage mates. This might not always indicate aggressive behavior between cage mates- accidents do happen. Keep an eye out for it though. You will have to go to the veterinarian for appropriate treatment of an eye injury like this.

Sugar Gliders can get cataracts just like humans. Symptoms include grey clouding of the eyeball and difficulty ascertaining their environment (you might notice it manifesting itself as your Sugar Glider being much more hesitant to glide somewhere). Some cataract formation is simply genetic disposition. The most common causes of cataracts unfortunately are malnutrition. Hypervitaminosis A (lack of vitamin A in the diet) and hyperglycemia both contribute to accelerated cataract formation in Sugar Glider eyeballs.

Chapter 12. Internet Resources

Ah, the internet! The internet is like a scalpel- it can work wonders in the right hands and horrors in the wrong hands. As you very likely already know, there is quite a bit of misinformation floating about the world wide web. What to do about it?

Beware online forums

Bottom of the totem pole for any information on the internet is any sort of discussion forum. This doesn't mean that the people writing on such forums are bad people, they may simply be misinformed. If you happen to come across a problem that has not been covered in this book, please research other books first. If you still have not found an answer you are pleased with, save it for your next trip to the veterinarian. I would only suggest taking advice from internet forums for trivial things (like what to name your Sugar Glider, etc.) that will be of no consequence to your pet.

If you happen to come across a forum member giving you what appears to be sage advice, please don't hesitate to ask them what their experience is. Do they have a reputable website? If they do, do they have any accreditation to back up their claims? A veterinarian sharing advice on their blog is miles ahead of some stranger in a chatroom who simply claim they have spent a lot of time with their pet Sugar Glider. General common sense guidelines can save you a lot of headaches.

Your veterinarian should be your first source

Despite what you read anywhere (books included), your veterinarian should be your most trusted source of information. The reason for this is that they will have your Sugar Glider in their hands in person - they have years of professional experience and can analyze a wide variety of variables quickly. Your Sugar Glider is unique anyway - there might need to be a deviation from standard protocol. As well as this, everything you read has to go through one dangerous filter: you. Don't take offense, but people misread things all the time, misunderstand ideas, etc.

By reading something from a trusted source and then running it by your veterinarian, you get at least two pairs of eyes on the same problem. If for whatever reason the advice your veterinarian gives you doesn't sit well with you, always feel free to get a second opinion! They are only human after all, and can make mistakes just like anyone else.

Googling
Google can be your best friend- if you know what you are looking for. When doing a general search, feel free to ask Google a generic question in the search box. If the results you have turned up don't satisfy you, consider more specific wording. For example, if you are looking up "what should a Sugar Glider nesting box look like" cut it down to "Sugar Glider nesting boxes"- this will cut out a lot of fluff. If your question is more academic in nature, Google has other resources than their general search engine to pull from. Google Books and Google Scholar are great resources and you can pull out very specific scientific and medical information from these resources.

All these Google resources are particularly useful for finding out if Sugar Gliders are even legal to possess in your particular jurisdiction (despite the thorough research the author has done throughout a variety of jurisdictions throughout the world). YouTube is also another useful Google resource- although this information tends to be more layman than anything else.

Sugar Glider Organizations you should know about

Note: at the time of printing, all these websites fully functioning. As the internet changes rapidly, some sites might no longer be live when you read this book. That is, of course, out of our control.

United States and Canada

Rescue Organizations
Suggiesavers
http://www.suggiesavers.org/
rescue@luckyglider.org

Based out of Texas, this organization has an exceptional wealth of information related to Sugar Gliders. They have an aggressive campaign on the Google AdWords (the ads you see during searching) network trying to spread the word that Sugar Gliders are *not* casual pets. A bona fide Non Profit 501c3 charitable organization with USDA licensing to hold Sugar Gliders, they are bar none *the* rescue organization for Sugar Gliders in the United States. They are always seeking *qualified* applicants to adopt out their rescued Sugar Gliders - so if adoption is the path you wish to go, reach out for them. This book will help you pass the exam they administer before they agree to let you have one of their precious rescues.

Many states have smaller rescue organizations dedicated to Sugar Gliders, or are more general rescue organization with Sugar Gliders to adopt out. Contact your local animal shelter as well, they may know of a Sugar Glider in need of a forever home.

Informational Organizations
Association of Sugar Glider Veterinarians
http://www.asgv.org

Also based out of Texas, the Association of Sugar Glider Veterinarians has a wealth of resources to explain everything that owning a Sugar Glider will entail. They also have an extremely informative series of videos (published in 2009) on YouTube - you should definitely give them all a watch. As well as providing information to the public at large, they also can refer you to a local veterinarian that specializes in the care and treatment of Sugar Gliders.

Suncoast Sugar Gliders
http://www.sugar-gliders.com/

Although a commercial organization specializing in the sale of niche Sugar Glider supplies - they provide a wealth of information at no charge to the wider public. Based out of Sarasota, Florida they have years of experience handling thousands of Sugar Gliders and they will probably already know everything that this book covers by heart. The owner is named Lisa, and if you are seeking a reputable opinion on where to acquire a Sugar Glider ethically, she is your best bet for information.

United Kingdom

Rescue Organization
Grace's Rest- Midland Exotic Animal Advice, Education and Rescue Service
http://www.gracesrest.co.uk

Based out of Coventry, West Midlands, England. They are an organization dedicated to the rescue and rehabilitation of exotic species in the United Kingdom. If you should need any advice about where to adopt a Sugar Glider, or if one is indeed suitable for you to adopt, give them a call first. They will also freely dispense advice for the care of your Sugar Glider.

Informational Organization
To be frank, the Sugar Glider community in the United Kingdom is quite a bit smaller than in the United States. This is only to be expected, as the

United Kingdom is a far smaller market for exotic pets than the United States. In this day and age, information travels across international boundaries, so an American website will suit your needs just as easily. If for whatever reason you have a precise question about Sugar Glider care, reach out to Grace's Rest- Midland Exotic Animal Advice, Education and Rescue Service. For more general inquiries, the Royal Society for the Prevention of Cruelty to Animals (RSPCA) is an advocacy group dedicated to the wellbeing of all animals. They can likely point you in the right direction when it comes to things such as where to buy appropriate supplies, if there are any local organizations adopting out Sugar Gliders or whom to contact to determine if keeping a Sugar Glider is legal in your exact jurisdiction.

Australia

Due to Sugar Gliders being native to Australia, there are a variety of organizations dedicated to their care and rescue. Being considered native wildlife as well, very often there are government resources and agencies responsible for the wellbeing of Sugar Gliders in their respective jurisdictions.

An excellent source of information nationally in Australia is the Department of Biodiversity, Conservation and Attractions (https://www.dpaw.wa.gov.au/), it is literally their job to point you in the right direction in regards to local wildlife. Again, Sugar Gliders being native to Australia also means there are unique legal hurdles to Sugar Glider ownership in the country. Some places have a very laissez-faire attitude about Sugar Glider ownership (with no restrictions), to moderate restrictions, to outright prohibitions. Please refer to the legality portion of this book, and of course, always check with your local authorities to make sure you have the most up to date information regarding legislation that could affect the right to keep a Sugar Glider as a pet. Regardless of the legality of Sugar Glider ownership, in nowhere in Australia are you permitted, as a layman, to capture Sugar Gliders from the wild, so don't bother asking!

Victoria
Marsupial Society
info@marsupialsociety.org.au

There is an excellent organization in this province called the Marsupial Society (http://www.marsupialsociety.org.au/keeping-marsupials.html). As you can imagine, they are bonkers about marsupial husbandry. There is a nominal fee for differing levels of membership (between $10 and $20- so hardly breaking the bank). They also keep up to date about the legal issues surrounding the husbandry of marsupials, should your interest branch out from Sugar Gliders to other pouched animals.

Northern Territory
Parks and Wildlife Commission of the Northern Territory
https://nt.gov.au/environment

The territorial government will help you out in regards to Sugar Gliders. Pet ownership is permitted, and they encourage you to help distressed, wild Sugar Gliders should you encounter them.

South Australia
Government of South Australia- Department of Environment, Water and Natural Resources
https://www.environment.sa.gov.au

The situation in South Australia is very similar to that of the Northern Territory- they are very amenable to helping you be a good and responsible Sugar Glider owner.

The Rest of Australia
With the exception of the Australian Capital Territory (where Sugar Glider ownership is legal with no restrictions) the rest of the provinces have such difficult restrictions on Sugar Glider ownership as to make it impossible to own them as pets. A few places even have outright bans. Again, legislation changes over time, so contact your local environmental authorities to keep up to date on this matter.

A word of advice
You may notice something missing from this list of internet resources. If it has not become glaringly obvious, you will notice that nowhere in the book is there information on where to *buy* a Sugar Glider. There is a very good reason for this. First of all, it is because there are no shortage of breeders that can be found all over the internet. Second of all, it is because to find a good breeder, you need to do your research! Ask hard questions, ask for information on lineages, ask for licensing when applicable, etc. There are a lot of unscrupulous breeders out there, some are even downright abusive.

Call any of the rescue organizations I have listed and they will have their fair share of horror stories to share with you. If during your search for your own personal Sugar Glider you happen to come across a deplorable breeder who ill-treats their Sugar Gliders, please do not hesitate to reach out to an appropriate rescue organization. They can provide information as to what steps to take next to rescue the Sugar Gliders, including exactly what to say to local law enforcement to make them take action, if it comes to that.

Also, whenever possible, please do not *buy* your Sugar Glider. Just like a puppy or a kitten, there is nothing wrong per se with buying your pet, just there are so many unlucky abandoned Sugar Gliders in the world, they could really use your help.

If you insist that you must buy a Sugar Glider though, spend time to adequately research the species first, then secondly, the breeder. It is a huge responsibility, but as with anything else, a little preparation goes a long way!

I hope you will enjoy your Sugar Glider pet. Good Luck!

Copyright and Trademarks: This publication is Copyrighted 2017 by Zoodoo Publishing. All products, publications, software and services mentioned and recommended in this publication are protected by trademarks. In such instance, all trademarks & copyright belong to the respective owners. All rights reserved. No part of this book may be reproduced or transferred in any form or by any means, graphic, electronic, or mechanical, including photocopying, recording, taping, or by any information storage retrieval system, without the written permission of the authors. Pictures used in this book are either royalty free pictures bought from stock-photo websites or have the source mentioned underneath the picture.

Disclaimer and Legal Notice: This product is not legal or medical advice and should not be interpreted in that manner. You need to do your own due-diligence to determine if the content of this product is right for you. The author and the affiliates of this product are not liable for any damages or losses associated with the content in this product. While every attempt has been made to verify the information shared in this publication, neither the author nor the affiliates assume any responsibility for errors, omissions or contrary interpretation of the subject matter herein. Any perceived slights to any specific person(s) or organization(s) are purely unintentional. We have no control over the nature, content and availability of the web sites listed in this book. The inclusion of any web site links does not necessarily imply a recommendation or endorse the views expressed within them. Zoodoo Publishing takes no responsibility for, and will not be liable for, the websites being temporarily unavailable or being removed from the Internet. The accuracy and completeness of information provided herein and opinions stated herein are not guaranteed or warranted to produce any particular results, and the advice and strategies, contained herein may not be suitable for every individual. The author shall not be liable for any loss incurred as a consequence of the use and application, directly or indirectly, of any information presented in this work. This publication is designed to provide information in regards to the subject matter covered. The information included in this book has been compiled to give an overview of the subject s and detail some of the symptoms, treatments etc. that are available to people with this condition. It is not intended to give medical advice. For a firm diagnosis of your condition, and for a treatment plan suitable for you, you should consult your doctor or consultant. The writer of this book and the publisher are not responsible for any damages or negative consequences following any of the treatments or methods highlighted in this book. Website links are for informational purposes and should not be seen as a personal endorsement; the same applies to the products detailed in this book. The reader should also be aware that although the web links included were correct at the time of writing, they may become out of date in the future.

www.ingramcontent.com/pod-product-compliance
Lightning Source LLC
Chambersburg PA
CBHW070425080426
42450CB00030B/1398